Messner Books by
Gary Paulsen and John Morris

CANOEING, KAYAKING AND RAFTING
HIKING AND BACKPACKING

GARY PAULSEN and JOHN MORRIS

Canoeing, Kayaking and Rafting

Illustrated by
JOHN PETERSON and JACK STORHOLM

 JULIAN MESSNER   NEW YORK

5551

Copyright © 1979 by Gary Paulsen and John Morris
All rights reserved including the right of reproduction in whole or
in part in any form. Published by Julian Messner, a Simon &
Schuster Division of Gulf & Western Corporation, Simon & Schuster
Building, 1230 Avenue of the Americas, New York, N.Y. 10020.

Manufactured in the United States of America

Design by Sue Crooks

Library of Congress Cataloging in Publication Data

Paulsen, Gary.
  Canoeing, kayaking, and rafting.

  Includes index.
  SUMMARY: A guide to the necessary equipment,
techniques, and safety rules for successful canoeing,
kayaking, and rafting.
  1. Canoes and canoeing. 2. Rafting (Sports)
[1. Canoes and canoeing. 2. Rafting (Sports)
3. Kayaks and kayaking] I. Morris, John,
joint author. II. Peterson, John. III. Storholm,
Jack. IV. Title.
GV783.P34   797.1'22   79-15075
ISBN 0-671-32949-9

To Art Vance

Contents

An Introduction to Watercrafting

Some thousands of years ago, a hollowed log was pushed out on a still lake, a crudely fashioned paddle was dipped in the water and the sport—or art—of watercrafting was born.

Just when that happened isn't important. It is enough that it happened.

The use of waterways for enjoyment—watercrafting—is virtually unlimited. All you need is you and a body of water, really—and for that reason it becomes a difficult sport to discuss. There are practically no rules which hold true for all aspects of watercrafting, except for some safety measures which will be covered later and which are vital. Just in the area of canoeing, for instance, it is nearly impossible to make a flat statement which holds true for all canoes or canoeing situations. No sooner have you said that canoes tip easily, which they used to, than you find that some new cargo canoes are being made so they'll not tip even if forced to the edge. Or just when you say that a good canoe can be found which costs a couple of hundred dollars a kit turns up for thirty-five, complete, and a man on the east coast is making genuine birchbark voyager canoes for six *thousand* dollars each.

There are so many different kinds of kayaks, for so many different purposes—even one designed specifically for hunting seals with a spear—that it's an almost endless task just establishing norms. And it doesn't end.

As few as three years before this book was conceived, there were actually no rubber rafts being made specifically for whitewater cruising. A watercrafter getting ready to make a rafting (corking) trip down a rough river either had to have a raft made specially—at enormous expense— or use a surplus navy survival raft: fun, but most certainly ill-designed for the purpose and sometimes downright dangerous. Now there are companies making rafts for all types of special uses, and some companies are even thinking of making rafts for specific rivers: the Snake, Colorado, Green, etc., and a raft manufacturer is already working on a specific raft for surfing.

What it boils down to obviously is that there is no way to generally introduce the sport of watercrafting. It's just too wide a field, too vast an area of enjoyment to treat in general terms.

There are many ways to enjoy watercrafting. You must decide which way suits *you* personally and then go to it, keeping in mind not just what you like but what's available in your area for use. It's difficult to realize dreams of a wild life of whitewater conquering when you live in an area of placid small lakes or wilderness rivers.

So, first decide what's available, then decide what you want to do with what you have, and finally, get your feet wet—whether it's in a canoe, a kayak or a raft. The one thing you don't have to consider too much is money. Surprisingly, it takes very little money to get good equipment (as long as you don't mind repairing, or building from kits). Believe it or not, it's possible to get a good, used, tired-but-fixable canoe for less than a tennis racket and a pair of tennis shoes.

As a last thought, and a serious one—there is only one actual dead-fast requirement before getting into water-crafting:

Learn to swim.

Not just a dog paddle, or "staying alive in the water," but totally relaxed, utterly familiar swimming—with a good-sized chunk of underwater ability to go with it. Be able to hold your breath, while moving, for at least thirty seconds or more and also be able to roll on your back two or three times while underwater, maybe throw in a somersault while rolling, before you ever sit in a canoe or kayak or raft.

Know the water, *know* swimming until you're like an otter. Work in a local pool or pond until water is a second environment for you; until it's another home.

Then, with proper life jackets, you're ready to truly enjoy watercrafting.

Getting Started;
You and the River Craft

Some people see whitewater cutting its wild way through granite and are driven to master these stony canyons. They won't rest until they have learned everything there is to know about controlling the wild waters, until they have shot a canyon and come out the bottom drenched and stunned by the suddenness of the experience.

Others prefer to explore hidden lakes and wilderness areas, backpacking and canoe-hiking and fishing back in to where there are no people and the northern pike seem to have been trained to take a spoon. And still others prefer a placid river, getting dropped several miles upstream and bobbing down for a day catching panfish or catfish.

With canoes, kayaks and rafts there's something for everyone, something for every mood. But getting started can be a problem. Questions seem to assail the beginner: Will it be difficult? What if I live in a city? Can I just jump into a canoe and take off? Or is all this really going to be a lot more work than fun?

Of course it doesn't ever have to be hard work—it's just that some good times take a little more effort than others.

Nor is it necessary to make a life-long commitment to watercrafting just to check it out and see if you're going to like it or not. Scan the Yellow Pages or get in touch with a sporting goods store for the name of a rental agency. It's usually pretty easy to find somebody with a pickup and a few canoes who will take you seven or eight miles upstream for a few bucks. Nudge the boat into the water and drift back home—you'll know before you get halfway there whether watercrafting is in your blood or not. On this kind of float trip you really don't have to know a bow from a stern. With a little experimenting you can find out how the paddle works and keep the canoe in the middle of the creek and your worst worries will be sunburn and mosquitoes—easily prevented with a long-sleeved shirt and repellent (Cutter's seems to work best). The point is that for a minimal expense in money and time, you get a classic chance to discover if you like the sport or not.

It can be that easy. And it's a good bet you'll like the idea of watercrafting and will want to get more involved.

Which still leaves the slightly thorny decision as to just *which* aspect of the sport you want—and that's a decision deserving further study.

Canoeing, kayaking or rafting? Part of the problem is knowing what to expect in the different areas of watercrafting. You can't really know what interests you until you know what they're like, what's going on.

Costs, of course, make a difference, and can vary a tremendous amount within any one of the three choices. Then, too, the experiences vary greatly.

We are bypassing the vital role rubber rafts play in ocean survival because it is not specifically a form of watercrafting. The same rule holds true for the insanity known as tubing—climbing onto an innertube and pushing off into whitewater. 2700 people a year die from drowning and a fair percentage of them drown because they were tubing. For that reason we choose not to promote tubing by discussing it, except to stress that *it should be avoided* because innertubes are not dependable and in many areas tubing has been (rightly) made illegal.

As to what the three craft can do, canoes, for instance, will—up to a point—take on fairly significant rapids. Not the wild whitewater of the western canyons, but some fairly rough-and-tumble streams have been conquered by standard canoes. Canoes are also very good for smaller lakes and the not-terribly-rough rivers. They are a versatile boat, for many different purposes, easy to master and with the capacity to open hitherto closed areas of wilderness enjoyment.

Rafts, on the other hand, are most appropriate on fast-running waters. On a lake the raft is a sluggish bull of a boat, suited for people who are out for sun and a lazy splash on a hot August afternoon. Shooting a massive canyon full of wild rapids brings explosive life to the bullboats and they can provide heart-stopping action.

The kayak is a special breed of boat. It comes into its own in whitewater, even though it's a canoe, sort of. People will tell you the kayak's lineage goes back to the early Eskimos who designed it for ocean hunting and fishing. But the truth is that the modern kayak has about as much to do with Eskimos as it does with a city mass-transit system.

Most kayaks are made of synthetics and most of them are designed for slalom or downriver racing (sports which will be covered later). While some of their features might interest an Eskimo, the new kayaks are far too specialized for you to whip between a pack of icebergs and start harpooning seals. It would be like putting a racehorse to a plow—although despite the racing features of the modern kayak (or perhaps because of them), they can be adapted to a form of wilderness touring that is both fun and challenging. The most important thing to remember about kayaking is that it is most decidedly *not* a part-time affair. Kayaking demands proper and adequate training, with a competent instructor, and it simply isn't a sport that can be jumped into easily—as both rafting and canoeing are. If you just buy any old kayak and a double-bladed paddle and hit a pond or lake you're going to spend some very uncomfortable minutes upside down trying to figure out what in blazes happened. It's possible that for pure excitement the kayak offers a slight edge—certainly it is the fastest and wildest of the three—but it also takes the most effort to understand and use correctly; don't jump into the needleboats lightly.

Many people start with canoes and work into kayaks, and then keep both boats and alternate depending on need at the time. And perhaps that holds the key to your personal selection of sport—examine your need.

Rafts are extremely limited in use—one-shot downstream runs, to be carried back up by car for the next run; fun, but specialized. Kayaks are more open, can tour wilderness—if a bit uncomfortably—but are still relatively narrow in scope and perform best in racing or slalom or whitewater situations. Canoes can be used more for general work, lakes and quiet rivers, exploring back-in wilderness areas, fishing, wild-ricing, and yet tend to be a bit unwieldy in truly rough whitewater—more of a workhorse.

Judge accordingly, based on your needs, but if you're in doubt at all it might be wise to consider the canoe as a start. It's easy to handle, forgiving of your mistakes.

No matter which kind of watercraft you ultimately decide on, the next step is the same: getting a boat. Which also might be called trying to get a whole lot of the best of something for nothing—or as little as possible.

Basically, there are about five different ways to come by the equipment you need to get into watercrafting: buy, rent, build, borrow or trade. At the outset let's gloss over renting and borrowing—both are dicy, chancy and for the most part self-defeating. In one you spend money and don't get to own a boat, in the other you might lose a friend by wrecking your borrowed boat in whitewater.

Trading is extremely limited, also, in that you must have something that a person willing to trade a boat needs. The odds against this are usually so high that it makes it nearly impossible to trade something else for the exact boat you want and/or need when you want it.

That leaves buying and building. Let's take the first one—buying. If you're flat rich, you can just go out and pick up the best canoe, kayak or raft for the purpose you have in mind—going by the guides later in the specific chapters—and start learning how to enjoy crafting.

Unfortunately, few of us are that rich. And even if you are, you should still apply the concept of discrimination in your shopping. It is possible, for instance, to spend fifty dollars and three hundred dollars and get exactly the same canoe or kayak just because you didn't shop around.

Before you consider buying new, you might want to examine the used market. Take a shot at the want ads, the bulletin boards in stores and laundromats, shopping sheets and swap-talks on the local radio station. There are millions of people with canoes, hundreds of thousands with kayaks, just waiting to sell what they have and move up. With a little care, it's possible to get essentially a new boat for a fraction of the cost.

As for judging used quality, it's relatively simple. First use your eyes. Carefully examine the boat you're considering, whether glass or aluminum or fabric or wood (we'll cover construction methods in the next chapter). If there is nothing glaringly wrong, no wild obvious bends or tears or broken-fixed areas on the hull—if it *looks* good, it probably *is* good. For now. That is, for the person just starting in watercrafting. It isn't necessary to be more critical at this stage. It's very hard to hide a defect in a canoe or kayak (rafts fall into a different category and will be discussed later).

So, if the boat floats, if the previous owner used it on the water, if you can afford it—it's a good deal. If it's broken in half or has a tear-rip down the belly you *still* might want it, except that you'll want it much, much cheaper and will have to figure in the time to repair it. (We'll be getting into detailed repairs later, too.)

A good thought on used equipment: the rule of thumb is that the tougher and more reliable the craft when it was new, the less experienced you have to be if you decide to buy it used. A good aluminum canoe made by a reputable manufacturer tends to be a better used buy than a home-made wood-and-canvas job which may or may not have been that well put together in the first place.

Another concept to remember if you're buying used: don't forget to dicker. Work around the price, try to get it down, and then see how much extra equipment—paddles, cushions, life vests—you can get thrown in for the initial price.

If you choose not to buy used, or have to buy new for one reason or another, some of the same rules apply. Stick with reputable equipment at the start. A canoe company that's been in business several years is more likely to give you a good unit than some guy with the magnetized letters stuck to his pickup door who keeps trying to see how much money you have. Just use common sense, *then* dicker and try to get extra equipment and a discount rate.

The main thing to remember about buying, whether it be new or used, is: don't hurry. Get the absolute most you can for the least amount of money. Do a little off-season shopping—a canoe in winter is much cheaper than a canoe in the height of the season in mid-summer. Check around, take your time, and get what you want—in the end you'll come out ahead by having spent the time.

Building your own, the final method of obtaining a canoe or kayak, usually means getting a kit and following instructions. It is nearly impossible to completely make your own from scratch—at least if you are new to the sport. Experienced hands can do it, and it's done often, but at the start, if you're going to build, stay with the kits— the old tried-and-true, simple, never-fail kits.

Kits for canoes and kayaks are relatively easy to construct, assuming you have even a smattering of hand-eye coordination, and can save almost unbelievable amounts of money. At the time of this writing, 1979, a work canoe of sixteen feet, basic shape, straight common keel, (keels discussed later), runs about $360.00, new, finished, in either aluminum or fiberglass. Said canoes will weigh about 75 pounds and furnish good service. At this same time, a wood-and-canvas canoe, sixteen feet, weighing about 75 pounds, covered with a layer of fiberglass for toughening, carrying the same size cargo, same keel— everything the same—can be built at home for $38.00. Flat. And it only takes about a week. True, they'll look a little less slick, but they will do just as much. And at a tenth the cost, the kit is hard to beat.

If you're going into rafting, it's best not to think about doing your own at home. There really aren't any usable kits, and the idea of cutting up a bunch of innertubes and gluing them together and then trying to take the product down a wild river . . . somehow just doesn't work.

CHAPTER 2

Canoes

In all shapes and sizes, canoes go back into the dimmest recesses of our past—and in some cases have remained unchanged for thousands upon thousands of years. Nor are these necessarily modest little boats. The American Museum of Natural History in New York has a dugout canoe, made from a single tree, measuring over sixty feet long, eight feet wide and five feet deep. It's like a ship. And in the islands of the Pacific there are huge, two-hulled canoes and some single-hull canoes with outriggers that are still doing sea duty, often under twin-sided sails and in heavy storms.

The reason that the canoe has been around so long, can be found all over the world, and has proved so indispensable, is that it is a good, basic design firmly set on the concept that if a certain modification will make it better, make it.

For that reason it's very difficult to pin down and define a canoe. In the south they are called *pirogues*, some places in the north call them *rice boats*, because they're used for harvesting wild rice. Some of them have square sterns, even though dictionaries persist in calling a canoe a "... long, light boat, narrow and pointed at both ends."

Within very broad limits it is possible to call all sorts of things canoes. There are sailing canoes, complete with dagger-boards and keels, and in Great Britain the "canoe" has a closed deck, much the way we normally think of kayaks. As a matter of fact, modern racing kayaks are something of a later version of the British canoe. And incidentally, during the Second World War, the British canoe doubled as a ship of war. Several of them went into battle against German ships and actually sank some large freighters by sneaking in and affixing charges to the huge hulls.

For purposes of this book, however, some of the wilder versions of the canoe will be dropped. We will concern ourselves for now with the generally accepted concept of a canoe as a thin, light boat, shallow draft, pointed at both ends and propelled by a paddle or set of paddles. Freight and war canoes can wait until you're an expert.

When Europeans landed in the Americas, they quickly discovered that for the rivers and lakes broken by rough rapids their own longboats were worse than useless. They couldn't be carried, broke easily and were hard to repair. The Europeans quickly adopted the Indian canoe, designed specifically for American waters. As those early Europeans did for nearly everything else, they gave the canoe parts European names. (See illustration.)

The front is the *bow*, the rear is the *stern*, the two sides are called the *gunwales* (pronounced "gunnels") because that is the location of cannon on warships. The width of the canoe at the widest point, or in the middle (*amidships*) is called the *beam*. The spreaders that hold the gunwales out are called *thwarts*; in building dugouts, thwarts of increasing size are used to actually spread the sides of

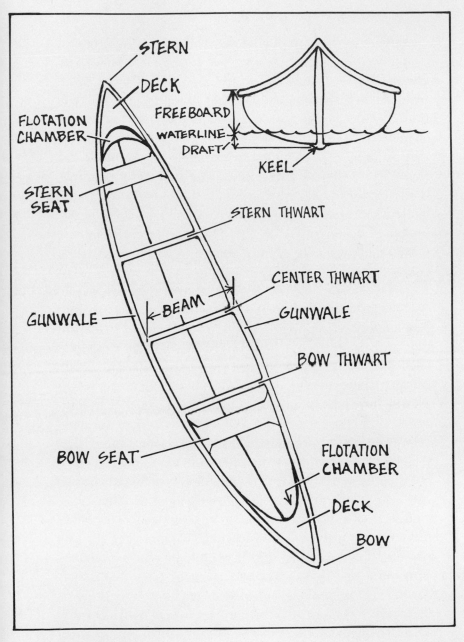

Parts of a Canoe

the dugout further and further apart: the wood is soaked in heated water and the sides pushed gently more and more apart to almost double the width of the original log. And that middle thwart, on your shoulders with the canoe upside down, is used for single-man portaging or canoe dancing.

All right, just a few more terms before getting down to cases. The *waterline* is the line along the canoe that the water comes to, and obviously the heavier the load the higher the waterline. The depth from the waterline to the bottom of the boat is called the *draft*, and from the waterline up to the top edge of the gunwale is called *freeboard*.

Finally, running underneath the length of the canoe is a kind of inverted dorsal ridge known as the *keel*. Keels do several things, but their main purpose is to keep the canoe from side-slipping in the wind or current. There are two kinds of keels, the lake keel and the shoe (or shallow) keel. The lake keel is deep and sharp and long and made for long, straight runs across wide bodies of water with possibly heavy loads. It is hard to turn a lake keel with any speed, and if you're getting a canoe for rivers or streams where you must turn fast, especially in whitewater, the shoe keel is the one you want. (See sketch.)

End of technical terms. Actually, they can be downright silly when some people get carried away with them. The truth is that to become an expert canoeist you don't *have* to know any of the terms in a technical sense, but for explaining things as we go it will be a help, and for talking with salesmen and the like it sometimes can be of assistance. But the terms themselves mean little, and the Indians, the inventors of the American canoe, used no such terminology to describe their boats.

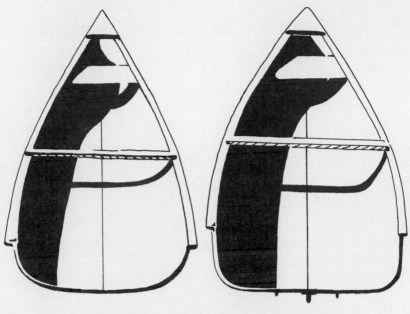

Shoe Keel   **Lake Keel**

What you *do* have to know before picking your own canoe is how to handle the problem of compromise in your desires. No single boat is going to fulfill all your needs, and so you become a canoeist with an uncertain air about half the time.

If you are only going to use your canoe in rushing water, and only use it alone, then what you want is the short (12 feet) boat with the shoe keel. Such a boat can easily be turned rapidly by one person, and is just as easily manhandled around on land, for car loading and off loading.

But that's it. If you want to take a couple of friends canoeing, especially on an overnight water-hike, you'll find the twelve footer much too short to take the extra loading. Or if you want to do a week or two of extensive lake or still water paddling, with long reaches and distances, the shallow keel will drive you mad trying to keep the boat moving in a straight line.

If you go for the big, 16–18 foot work canoes for fishing or long treks, it's almost mandatory to go with the aluminum so you can carry it. But aluminum has a tendency to "ripple" over long periods—get covered with small bumps and ridges—and these will actually cause a serious drag. Glass springs back from each little nudge, and works better in that respect, but is heavier to horse around with or carry.

Compromise. Again and again it is necessary to pick something you sometimes won't want to get something you sometimes *will* want.

Perhaps the best approach is to stop before you get committed to a course of action, back up a bit and reevaluate canoes and their construction methods.

First, it's necessary to simplify your thinking somewhat. As one oldtimer who works a trapline in northern Minnesota told us: "There's just two kinds of canoes—long and short."

As we have already seen, it's a bit more complicated than that, but the saying illustrates the right kind of thinking. Compromising aside, it's important to boil your thinking down to basic needs. There are, for you personally, only two kinds of canoes: the kind you want, and the kind you don't. Period.

If you are going to do whitewater a lot, or fast waters with a shallow bed and rocks and lots of turns—if you are anticipating working alone a great deal, exploring alone—then a short canoe is what you need. Twelve feet or even a bit shorter, with a shoe keel that allows rapid turns around those big donies, huge rocks, that seem to block the whole middle of the stream.

If you are going to work alone, but live in an area of quiet water and lakes, a twelve footer with a deep keel for long, straight runs is the way to go. Careful loading can turn the short boat into a fairly decent workboat.

On the other hand, if you anticipate being with a friend during most of your exploring or trekking, you have to go for a longer boat: fourteen to sixteen feet would be about right. And if it's going to be used on lakes, the deep keel; if rapid water, the shoe keel.

The choices go on. If you want a heavy workboat, capable of taking large cargoes (wild rice, fishing and trapping or long exploring supplies) the boat will have to have a fairly good beam and high gunwales. This will provide additional stability as well as load-carrying capabilities.

Or if you intend working an area where there will be a lot of long portages, you must reexamine the shorter canoes because they are easy to carry alone. Or conversely, if you will not be alone, the long one will work out all right because there will be two people to carry it.

Stay flexible, keep your mind open to all the possibilities of all the different kinds of things you'll be using your canoe for—not just a one shot trip, but for as long as you have it. A good canoe can easily last a lifetime, so you're looking at a long term project.

Of course it's definitely possible that you simply can't predict all the things you will be doing, and that brings us to the real meat of canoe selection—the all-purpose boat. The one canoe for all purposes, all seasons—the ultimate compromise.

Unfortunately, experts tend to disagree almost violently on just what this all-purpose boat should be. Some say short, others long; some say narrow, others scream wide, for possible heavy loads. It can, at best, present a very confusing picture because what we're after here is nothing less than a mythical boat. Allboat. Superboat. And in a very real way it can't exist.

But we can come up with a boat that comes close on several fronts, and will get the job done: a kind of work-horse that can run pretty fast, or a fast runner that can pull a heavy load—the Inbetweenboat.

A 14–16 footer seems to work out best. Go for the intermediate keel, deeper but short, not running the full length of the boat. And get a canoe that's fairly beamy, somewhere close to 35″ at the middle or widest point. Finally, look for a canoe that has a slight upsweep on both ends. This will make it turn a little faster in rough water. It will also be harder to control in wind on a lake—but later we'll talk of loading to compensate for that problem. Also, get a canoe that has fairly steep sides—not a big, shallow curve but more out from the keel and straight up, which gives you more stability and better load-handling characteristics.

Such an Inbetweenboat won't win races, or perform in wild whitewater as well as the specially designed models. But it will furnish years of all purpose service, hours and days of unbelievable challenge and fun, and get you on the water with a minimum of expense or work.

The boat just described is quite common. With any luck

Traditional Wooden Canoe

at all you can probably find a used one at a decent price
. . . Once you settle on the material the boat is constructed
from, of course. Material is almost as important as the kind
of canoe you select.

For all practical purposes there are only four basic materials used in the construction of canoes: wood, aluminum,
fiberglass, and wood-and-canvas. Skins used to be used
quite a lot, especially in Eskimo boats, but are rarely used
anymore.

Of the four materials, wood is also becoming more and
more rare in boat construction. If you are considering an
old all-wood canoe (there are virtually no new ones), there
are a few things to keep in mind. They are, if kept up,
stunningly beautiful things, especially if clear varnished
and shellacked. The wood is so rich and deep and alive
that it almost hurts to look at it. But the maintenance is
crippling. You are *always* sanding and varnishing and
shellacking and sanding and varnishing and sanding and
sanding . . . and that's just for starters. Wood has to be
"wetted-in," soaked to swell the little boards to stop leakage, and then stored up on a rack for the winter to keep it
straight and dried properly. On the water it will probably
still leak just a bit, so you need a baling cup or sponge.
And, finally, wood canoes gain weight all summer: the
wood soaks up water. On a long, or even short, portage
this extra weight can be murderous, can really drag you

down, literally. Wood canoes are very much a love-hate kind of relationship and you'll find people clucking with envy when they see you even as they shake their heads in pity. Wood is for the purist.

Moving up the ladder of convenience we come to wood-and-canvas. These come in kit form. We made one for research, a 16-footer from Trailcraft, and it peformed admirably. It leaked very slightly, but when we laminated a layer of glass cloth to the canvas even this leakage stopped.

The idea of these boats is to cover a light wood skeletal structure with a fabric that becomes waterproof with repeated coats of paint. The idea is very old, but still works well enough to demand consideration.

All instructions come with the kits, are easy to follow, and the boats very easy to make. And they do not have the disadvantages of the pure wood boats. With proper painting they don't gain weight, nor do they require the massive maintenance program. In a few years, if the canvas or canvas-and-glass wears away, it can be easily replaced with a new "skin" for just a few dollars and an afternoon of work.

If money is a consideration, it might be a definite plus to take a look at the canvas-and-wood model. They are much tougher than you might think when the concept is first presented to you. The rib and cloth and strip construction makes them flexible and strong, and the simplicity of materials makes them easy to repair. Also, they are just flatteningly inexpensive—a *good* 16-footer goes for under fifty dollars, at the time of this writing. Complete.

The two materials left are the most popular, the kinds you see everywhere: aluminum or straight fiberglass. Of the two, aluminum is—or was—the most popular, but its popularity is fading a bit as glass improves.

Older glass canoes had hand-layed-up hulls and were fair brutes for weight. They were very tough and could take staggering amounts of punishment. But they were hard to lift and carry and you started off with a kind of workhorse feeling. People bought glass for working, for wild-ricing, for duck hunting, for long trips on lakes; and they bought aluminum for everything else.

But modern glass canoes are comparable in weight to aluminum. New materials, new techniques have improved the strength-to-weight ratio of glass so that it is about the same as aluminum. Glass also holds its color better, doesn't dent or "ripple," and doesn't emit that tinny "clinker" sound so annoying to fishermen trying to remain silent. (Incidentally, certain sounds actually *do* scare fish. Any sharp sound does, but the "clinker" sound seems to drive them off further.) The disadvantages of glass (which includes all new fabrics and synthetic lay-up materials) are that it fades in luster over a couple of years, and it tends to get abraded on sandy or gravel bottoms. Except for appearance, the color doesn't matter, but the abrading can be a problem, although it can be repaired easily enough.

The most decided advantages to glass are that it "flexes" to take shock—you can sometimes literally see it move. And its flexibility allows it to be made into more favorable shapes.

Now for aluminum. Its only advantage over glass is its lightness. Although some of the new balsa-wood-and-fiberglass sandwich canoes are also light, it's still true that aluminum is the lightest. Aluminum also tends to require less care—you needn't store it, it won't rot (neither will glass) and it doesn't need repainting (largely because it's nearly impossible to get a coat of paint to stick to it).

But right about there the advantages start disappearing

5551

and the disadvantages come to the surface. Because paint *won't* hold, the stuff shines sun in your eyes—and it can be maddening to spend a few days on water with that shine kicking into your face. And it can burn.

Aluminum also dents, and "ripples," as already discussed, and that, too, can slow you down a bit over the long haul—for hard work, exploring, seeing the back country. Along with the denting, prolonged use of aluminum canoes in rough water can lead them to "loosen" slightly—the rivets work a bit loose—and they can leak. True, all of these problems can be fixed, and methods of repair will be discussed in the repair section, but they can put a damper on enthusiasm. And repair of damage, a tear or massive dent, is more difficult to do well with aluminum than other materials. Unless you're an expert in metal work, it's possible for the fix to look a little hinky. The water will stay out, but that's about it.

In the end the only true advantage to aluminum is probably that it's the most inexpensive kind to buy used. Because they are the most popular, or were, there are used aluminum canoes all over the place and it's likely that you can find one in fair shape for a very good price.

A precautionary note: when buying canoes, either glass or aluminum, beware of former rental canoes. The large rental resort-type places periodically sell off their canoes—as do camps and the like—and you can sometimes find a fair deal. But caution is the word. Those rental and camp canoes take unbelievable punishment. Don't buy, don't even start to buy, until you have given the canoe an extremely careful examination, both *out of* and *in* the water.

In glass canoes look especially for "starring," where the surface of the canoe looks kind of shattered in little pockets, usually on the outside. This is caused by heavy blows, or jumping into the canoe wrong, or throwing heavy objects into the canoe, and can lead to soft spots in the hull which might later leak and cause trouble.

Get aluminum canoes in the water and check for leaking. Hard wear loosens the rivets, and although they can be fixed, as we've said, it might get the seller to bring the price down if the thing leaks.

None of these things need stop you; they can all be fixed, but know about them in advance for your own good.

The only kind of canoe to truly avoid—other than a rotted-out wood or canvas canoe—is one in which the whole canoe is warped. Here again aluminum is usually the villain, but it can also happen to glass and wood or wood-and-canvas. What happens is that the canoe is subjected to a tremendous lateral shock, a twisting motion, and the hull is permanently twisted and warped out of shape. The two things which cause this most are improper use in whitewater, or the boat falling off the top of the car at high speed. The way to see it is simply to stand at one end of the canoe with the boat sitting either flat on the ground or level in the water. Align the points, the bow and stern sticking up, and if they don't align, or won't align properly, don't buy the canoe. Period. A warped canoe will drive you crazy trying to keep it moving in a straight line—or even a curve. They go everywhere but where you want to go, and they aren't worth the headaches no matter how cheap they are.

What you're trying to achieve by buying a canoe is a new kind of freedom, a new latitude for self-expression. And if what you wind up with is a clunker of a boat that keeps you slamming back and forth with a paddle all the time, the whole thing becomes self-defeating.

Don't buy desperately, buy to suit your needs. Get the canoe *you* need. And the same holds true for the next step: getting equipment.

CHAPTER 3

Gear for Getting Started

There is a tendency, sometimes downright disastrous, to gloss over the equipment needed to get onto the water. The canoe is there, probably just what's needed and wanted, and you just pick up a couple of paddles at the nearest discount store and head out for the wilderness with a couple of sandwiches in your pocket and all the world out ahead of you.

In a way it's possible to have a limited kind of fun that way—just get a cheap paddle and gig around on the nearest lake or big pond. And perhaps for many that's enough.

But if a bit of care is taken in selecting equipment and getting your canoe ready to go, it can mean a dramatic increase in the amount of fun you can have. That care can also save unbelievable amounts of fatigue over the months and years you'll be using your canoe. And it can help you avoid trouble and even possible danger.

CANOE PADDLES

Paddles are, obviously, what makes a canoe move across the water. But more, the canoe paddle becomes an exten-

sion of yourself; over the many thousands of times you
will use the paddle—stroking the boat, turning it, stopping
it, pushing off danger, balancing in precarious positions—
during all this, the paddle is where you meet the water,
the direct link between the canoeist and the boat and the
water. Small wonder that the *voyageurs* of the north had
whole dances built around the paddle as well as the
canoe—graceful wheeling motions. They still have the
dances at various Canadian festivals and they are a joy
to see, if you get the chance.

The paddle is an important part of the canoeing experience. And yet many people slide over getting their paddles
too lightly.

Under no condition buy *any* paddle until you have held
it in your hands, felt what it's like, seen if it "fits." That is
the first, the most important stipulation. Don't buy it if it
doesn't feel right, blade, stem and spade handle grip.
You will be using the paddle for many hundreds of hours,
and if it seems a little off at first, it will only get worse. Go
through a whole rack of paddles, if need be, one at a time,
until you find one that feels right, then keep it in your
hand for a while to make sure it works. If it does, take
it home and don't loan it to anybody. Ever. The right
paddle is that important.

As to length—it depends on what you're going to be
doing. If it's your canoe, you will probably be sitting
mostly in the stern. In that case you'll want the paddle
about eye level. Just put the tip on the floor and stand
next to it—if the grip comes in at about eye level, you're
all right. A half inch or so isn't critical.

On the other hand, if you figure to do most of your
work in the bow of somebody else's canoe, you'll want the

paddle just a bit shorter. The grip should reach about the mouth or chin, but again it isn't critical. What *is* critical is how the paddle feels—don't get it if it feels odd.

As for the kind of paddle, the material, it's hard to beat laminated wood. There are some synthetic paddles being made, especially for kayakers, but for canoeing the old-fashioned flat-bladed, laminated wood paddle works best and also seems to be the least expensive.

Look down the paddle to make sure it's straight before you buy it. If there is a warp, and the paddle veers in one direction or the other, it can be fatiguing in a day of paddling. Your shoulders will ache from constantly trying to compensate for the error.

Also check to make certain the laminated sections are firmly glued together. This goes for new as well as used paddles.

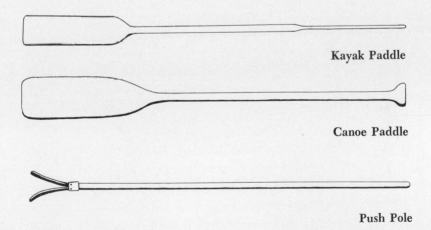

Kayak Paddle

Canoe Paddle

Push Pole

Finally, on any wood paddle, get a half pint of spar-varnish and a small brush, and before you put the paddle in the water give it a quick coat. Like everything else these days, the work on some of those paddles can be a little shoddy—they never seem to get quite enough varnish and the water can work through into the wood. Over an extended period this could lead to warping, and soaking of the wood which will make the paddle slightly heavier. This "slightly heavier" begins to take on importance on a long portage, where every pound takes on the weight of an anvil.

Before giving the paddle that coat of varnish, take some very fine sandpaper or coarse steel wool and rub the paddle down. This will remove any grit left from previous finishes, and prepare the surface of the wood so the varnish adheres better. Use a tack rag to get rid of any remnants of your sanding or any other dirt before you varnish.

LIFE VESTS

Some people persist in canoeing without life vests, which amounts to nothing less than a foolish risk of life. Even for the totally competent swimmer, accidents happen. Horror stories abound concerning people who can swim, are very good at swimming, and yet drown because the edge of the boat stunned them, or they hit a rock, or the shock of the cold water made them panic.

If you're considering any kind of watercraft, get a good life vest and wear it.

As for the quality of different vests, some caution is needed. It isn't that vest manufacturers are necessarily unscrupulous, but the truth is that it's quite possible to buy a new life vest that doesn't do the job—won't hold you up. For all the obvious reasons this is worse, in a way, than no vest at all—just when you need to depend on the thing, you go down like a brick. Also, there are certain kinds of so-called flotation devices which float you wrong side up—the waist-belt can do this. And whipping down a river with your head down and bottom up is most decidedly *not* fun watercrafting.

So get a good vest, either foam or plastic covered kapok. Get it in a visible color (orange, international-bright). Make certain the vest is Coast Guard approved. There will be a little tag on the vest saying so. And then go to the nearest pool and try it. Fall into the deep end from a sitting position, on your back, sideways, all the ways which might approximate the way you'd fall from a canoe accidentally. Make certain that (a) the vest holds you up in a totally relaxed condition and (b) it is self-righting. Even if you go into the water upside down on your back the vest should roll you over and bring you to the surface with your face up.

If it doesn't, if it floats you incorrectly, or any way but on your back with your face up, if for *any* conceivable reason you find the vest doesn't work, or you don't like it, take it back at once, get a different one and test again. There can be no compromise.

CUSHIONS, KNEEPADS

Flotation cushions are nice to have around for several reasons. For one, you can never have enough floating gear; if the canoe tips, no, *when* the canoe tips (they all do eventually), it's good to have things to grab. Even wearing your life vest. But more important, now and then you'll want to just sit in the canoe—perhaps to fish. And no part of any canoe is soft and/or comfortable to sit on or in. The cushions earn their keep the first afternoon you sit pulling in sunfish or bluegills, leaning back in soft comfort.

Kneepads are also worth the money they cost, but only if you're racing or going to do some long cruising for extended periods of paddling-time. Otherwise, for general use, a cushion will be more comfortable.

If you feel you need kneepads, first try the hardware store or lumberyard. Check out a pair of cement worker's kneepads, also known as roofer kneepads. They're just as good, maybe a little tougher, and probably won't cost half as much as the "official" canoe kneepads. The same holds true for elbow pads, which are very helpful in heavy whitewater situations. Check the local sporting goods store for football elbow pads. They'll work just as well as the more expensive canoeing pads.

HELMETS

Whitewater demands a helmet, a *proper* helmet, and here there can be no shortcutting. Nor are there any substitutes for a boating helmet. If you try to get by with a football helmet, you'll find it filling with water and holding your head down. Get a good, approved, boating helmet if you anticipate doing any whitewater at all; those underwater rocks can be vicious if you turn turtle.

MISCELLANEOUS GEAR

Actually if you intend doing any lengthy cruising, it's possible to get completely wrapped up in odds and ends of canoeing gear. There is so much you can use, of such a wide variety, that pinning things down is like trying to grab a cloud of mosquitos.

But for general use, for getting a good start, there are a few basic supplies which can help make things easier. At the very top of the list should come mosquito and fly repellent. No matter where you are, mosquitos or biting flies can wreck your fun. More, they can come in such unbelievable numbers and with such ferocity that they can all but drive you insane. This is especially true in the north country, up in the northern reaches of Minnesota or in the lakes of southern Ontario. They have literally driven men and moose mad with their bites, and there are several cases of moose being weakened to the point of death by loss of blood from the mosquitos and flies. It's been said before, but it bears repeating: carry repellent, always.

As far as types go, research done for this book found the Cutter's stick to be the longest lasting and seemingly most effective—at least in Minnesota. You rub it on exposed skin and it holds for three to four hours, unless washed off. However, it was found that what worked really well in northern Minnesota didn't faze the biting flies in Lake Powell, Utah; spray worked better there. So be sure to take two or three different brands and types— liquid, spray, or stick—with you in strange country so you have effective protection.

The sun can be devastating, so take a good floppy hat

or cap and some sunburn cream. If you're prone to dry or chapped lips, they'll probably react to canoeing a bit, so use some kind of lip protection. The sun is really vicious on a still day. Because you're so low to the water, it seems to reflect like hot bullets; and if you burn a little normally, you'll absolutely scorch in a canoe. Wear long-sleeved, white, loose shirts and keep a little zinc oxide around to protect your nose. A note on sunburn: canoeing brings a burn out in a place not usually burned, namely the soles of bare feet. It might sound humorous, but nothing is as painful as burning the tender soles of your feet—it's an active pain and lasts a long time. So wear tennis shoes, or at least socks.

Besides bugs and sun there is really nothing uncomfortable waiting for you, but a couple of handy things to have around can keep you functioning on a convenient level. First, throw about twenty feet of cheap nylon rope on the bow of the canoe, just tied with a double or triple knot. No matter the kind of canoe, you'll find a rope hole or fixture on the bow. If you build your own, work a brass eye into the bow, as per the plan. This rope, inexpensive and easy to put on, can save hours of hassle. When you stop on shore just tie the end to the nearest stump or tree or limb and leave the canoe in the water. Otherwise, every time you pull that boat up onto the ground, you grind a little off the bottom; even on grass there will be rocks. But if you tie it and leave it in the water, the bottom will stay smooth, and wear will be kept to a minimum. Repairing an abraded canoe bottom is a terrific amount of work. It can be done, except on aluminum, but it takes a long time. Use the rope.

The other quickie item which can make things work a

little better is to pick up a few of those elastic stretch
cords with the hooks on either end. Just wrap them
around the seats or hook them from one thwart to the
next and forget them. Then, when you have supplies or
equipment in the canoe—spare paddle (necessary on long
trips), or camping gear, fishing gear, clothing, even a
quick lunch—wrap an elastic cord around it and tie it
down. If/when you go over, you won't lose it.

There will be other, specialized, on-boat equipment
discussed later in the chapter on exploring or taking long
trips, but the above will get you started with a maximum
of ease and safety and a minimum of discomfort.

One more thing before getting down to putting the
canoe into the water: specifically, getting the canoe *to*
the water.

Unless you live right on a river or lake, it's likely you
won't have instant, or even easy, access to water for
canoeing. Of course, this means you'll have to transport
the canoe, and the classic method of transportation is the
car-top carrier. Buying one of the things just for carrying
your canoe is to be avoided. The official canoe carriers are
ridiculously expensive for what you get, and do no better
than one you can make or jury rig.

If you already have a ski rack, car-top variety, it will
work just as well. Just center the canoe on top of the rack,
tie a short tie on each side to the thwarts, and bring
ropes down to the front and rear bumpers. Tie the front
and rear especially tight because the canoe will "roam"
in the wind created by driving; work its way back and
forth.

If you haven't a ski rack or other car-top device, it's
easy to make one. First use cushions to protect the car

and canoe from damage. Make two canvas tubes 40 inches long by 6 inches wide. Any cloth will work, but canvas is tougher. Use the sewing machine to sew up the sides and one end, as illustrated. Then pack the tubes with a good filler that has some give—sawdust, little styrofoam cubes, wood shavings, anything that is lightweight and works. When the cushions are full and quite firm, tie off or sew up the end.

These two tubes lie across the width of the car, spaced to keep the canoe from touching the top. They can be adjusted to fit any car or station wagon. Tie the boat to the front and rear bumpers, and bring short ropes down on either side from the center thwart to keep the canoe from moving side to side.

This arrangement allows the canoe to ride upside down on its gunwales on top of the car, and the cushions can easily be stored on a shelf in the garage when not in use.

The tube-pads also make a handy portaging pad across the shoulders for protecting the neck and back on long portages. This sort of thing isn't truly needed, but on long

Diagram for Car-Top Cushions

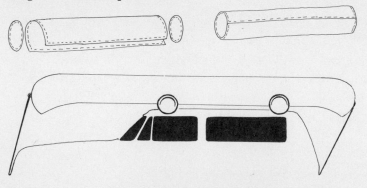

Cushions in place, extending beyond canoe and top of vehicle

hauls or explorations it can ease the muscles and make the trip a bit more enjoyable. The tubes also double fairly well for pillows; and if you use styrofoam cubes for the stuffing they make decent emergency flotation devices. When stowing in the canoe, tie them beneath the seats and they'll supplement the flotation safety factor built into the canoe. This gives you a nice edge of safety if the canoe is heavily loaded and you go over in rough water or waves.

CHAPTER 4

Canoeing; Getting Wet

There are many schools of thought on different methods to approach canoeing. Some say it's necessary to take a course somewhere, perhaps at a summer college or summer school, before you're entirely qualified to take off in a canoe. Others think you should spend some hours in a small pond or "tame" pool of shallow water to start.

In truth, both methods are okay—but a bit much. However, they do point up the single step that must be taken to get started, to wit: it is necessary to mix you, the canoe, and some water at the outset. Later there can be finesse, and perhaps even professionalism, but at first just you, the canoe and water.

Wear a swimming suit. Pick a warm day. Ease into the canoe from a dock. Settle your weight in the middle of the bottom, drift a bit away from the dock and roll over.

Take the canoe all the way over. Right at the start. Before you learn anything else, before you start paddling, before you fish or explore or even move the boat—take it over. Just take one gunwale in each hand and start leaning until the boat capsizes.

Stay with the canoe. *Don't* touch the dock. You'll see

47

that the boat continues to float, that it will actually hold you up, even full of water. All canoes have flotation, and the safest thing to do when you tip is stay with the boat. Always.

What we are practicing here is the ultimate mixing of the ingredients. Tipping is the maximum expression of distress you will probably experience with the canoe. By doing it right off, you learn that it isn't serious, that indeed it only amounts to a dampening experience and you needn't panic or even get alarmed.

Also, and more critical, by tipping you'll know exactly how far you can go with your personal canoe. You'll know the point of no return and—assuming you're new to canoeing—you should also find that they're much harder to tip than you initially thought. As a matter of fact, if your canoe has a slight belly that curves from front to back and up gently at both ends, it's downright hard to get it to go over. What happens is that the canoe hits stable points as you lean, stabilizing at each little place, until the edge goes under and the canoe gently fills with water and submerges. It will go down until it floats flush with the surface of the water, and there it will stay.

Getting back into the canoe is a reversal of the tipping procedure. First tip the canoe side up in the air, kind of roll it up by pushing down on the side nearest to you, so that it rolls the water out. (See sketch.)

Once the canoe is reasonably empty—it will never empty completely but have a trace of water in the bottom—you must pull yourself back in. It's not too difficult. Just reach up and across the middle of the canoe and belly yourself carefully up until you are lying across, your legs in the water, balanced on the gunwales. (As in the illustration.)

Rolling the water out

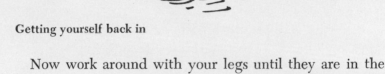

Getting yourself back in

Now work around with your legs until they are in the canoe, and sit down on the bottom. It's really that easy. In fact it's a good idea once you're wet anyway just to tip the canoe a few times, five or six, empty it, and get back in, until it's easy for you. It's well worth the effort it takes, and it might save you a bunch of problems later because it will help you truly know yourself and your canoe.

Once you have mastered tipping and emptying and getting back in, once you are totally familiar with the canoe, go back to the dock. Practice getting in and out from the dock a few times, balancing your weight equally on the two gunwales in the middle. Get in one foot at a time, balancing your weight in the middle.

Do not try any of the fancy entries you may have seen in movies or heard others talking about. Don't run and jump in and glide on out the way they seem to show in every old Indian movie. This can result not just in tipping, but in damage to the bottom of the canoe. Loading in a canoe must be spread over a broad area. Sudden weights in small areas can damage the hull.

Again, as with tipping, get in and out a dozen or so times. Do it until the whole maneuver is thoroughly familiar to you, until you can do it without that high-unbalanced feeling in your throat or a lot of wobbling or shaky wiggling.

What we're doing with these basic steps is getting them out of the way so they don't trip you up later. If you know all about tipping, and getting in and out, you'll know about balance in the canoe. It will make everything smoother as you go.

After you've got it all straight, loading or getting in and tipping, sit in the canoe and push it to various points short of tipping, until you know all those points. Then try getting into the boat incorrectly. Step off center, grab one gunwale, gig around—really *know* what's going to happen when you goof. Then, when you make a mistake it won't mean the end of the enjoyment for you.

With firm knowledge of the canoe and your reaction to it, the next steps are sitting in your canoe, and moving it across the water.

SITTING IN THE CANOE

There are several considerations to take into account as to placement of your body in the canoe. Some sit up on the seat for comfort—and this is especially nice for fishing or duck hunting. But it does raise the weight in the canoe, reduces stability, and for that reason many prefer kneeling in front of the rear seat, lowering the center of gravity.

Kneeling is mandatory, obviously, in rough water or white-water.

Another consideration involves wind. If you're in the stern of the canoe, and paddling alone, the front end of the canoe cambers up in the air, sort of rocks up. If there is a stiff wind, common on lakes, that front end will catch the wind like a weathervane and it is impossible to turn the canoe into the wind as you should. You can paddle as fast and as hard as you want, but the wind will push that nose around and you can't win. What you must do in this case is move your body forward to rock the nose back down. If the wind is truly strong you might have to sit near the middle of the canoe—assuming again that you're alone and there is no cargo to load in front.

If somebody is with you, of course, all this changes. You already have weight in front to hold the nose down so wind isn't the vital problem that it is when you're alone. But balance is a bit more of a problem because with two people you have just that much more weight above the center of gravity. For that reason when two people are canoeing it's a good idea to start by kneeling until you are both more experienced. Both parties kneel in front of their seat.

PADDLING CANOES

Basic Strokes

If you're working alone, the classic paddling position is in the rear, reaching forward and pulling back. This time it *is* the way you see it in films.

And that method will work. It will drive the canoe forward across the water, a silent slipping ghost of grace and beauty. And before you read any further, before you consider any other part of canoeing, it is important to realize that this first stroking, this first movement, is all you *have* to know to enjoy canoeing. There is much more that can be known, knowledge which will make it all more full and rich as an experience; but for now, *all* you need is this first knowledge: tipping, getting in and out and first movement.

You can live with that for the rest of your life. You can get around on that, have a good time, do limited exploring, some fishing, the close-in work that a canoe does so well. That's one of the beautiful things about canoes. Unlike kayaks, which demand more knowledge, a canoe will serve well with minimal skill and time spent to learn.

If, however, you'd like to smooth the work a bit, and expand your abilities, the canoe will allow that, too, and will expand with you—it is nearly unlimited.

Take paddling. Just using the basic stroke, reaching ahead and pulling back, will move the canoe. But if you advance the forward reach a bit by leaning forward when you reach out, keeping your lower arm straight and the paddle straight up and down as you pull it back, you'll find your speed almost doubling for only a little more work.

Also, by paddling on one side you find that the canoe turns. You have to keep changing sides, and this can get wearying after a few hours. So instead you learn to change your stroke, pulling straight back and kicking it out a little to the side at the end to keep the canoe moving on the same course, straight and true, without you changing sides all the time. (As illustrated.)

After you get the basic movement down, all the strokes and improvements can be accomplished on a good base. Some of the variations in methods are listed below, but re-

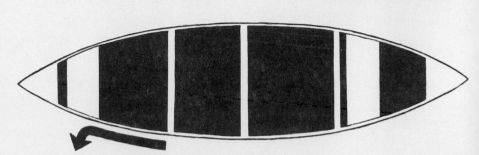

Arrows show paddle movements for kicking out

member that they are suggestions only. If your way works better for you, by all means use it—staying flexible is the name of the game.

Clawing Strokes

There are times when you want to turn rapidly, either to avoid a dangerous obstruction or to maneuver in a small area. To do this, you use a clawing or reaching stroke. These are strokes which essentially move the canoe end sideways while causing very little forward motion.

Just reach out with your paddle in the direction you wish to go, and pull the water towards you. This forces the canoe to move sideways in the direction desired. It's that simple.

Back Stroking

Obviously done when you want the canoe to move backwards, the back-stroke does exactly as the name indicates. You just paddle backwards by reversing the forward process.

If you wish to add a bit of strength to this normally weak stroke, put the weight of your shoulder into the stroke on the propelling backwards portion—kind of lean down on the paddle as you push back. It adds a bit of muscle to it and is especially handy when you're trying to back out of thick weeds or when your bottom is stuck on lily pads, both common in the north country.

Kick-Out Stroke

For a sudden push sideways of the end of the canoe, when for one reason or another a clawing or reaching stroke can't be done, the kick-out stroke is easy.

You merely jam the paddle down flat against the side of the canoe and pull back on the top, using the gunwale and side of the canoe as the fulcrum of a lever.

Sculling Stroke

This is a stroke which is popular, or at least talked about a lot, and which is virtually useless because other strokes accomplish more for less effort.

What you do is keep the blade of the paddle in the water, set it at an angle and move it gently back and forth. It's supposed to move the canoe silently across the water, but what it really does is get you tired and accomplish nothing. Or very little.

Silent Stroke

For wildlife photography, or fishing in those hidden places, or duck hunting, now and then a silent stroke is necessary.

When the paddle is taken out of the water it causes a noisy splash. To stop this, obviously, the paddle must be left in the water. Just take the normal stroke, and when it's finished, instead of taking the paddle out of the water, turn it sideways so the sharp edges face forward and back, and push the paddle easily and slowly forward. When the paddle is in position for the next stroke, again turn it sideways and pull it back, moving the boat forward. This same stroke can be done with the paddle out at an angle, so that you can crouch over in the boat for close-in stalking. Perhaps needless to say, it must be done slowly and as gently as possible for maximum silence.

Steering Stroke

While actually not a true stroke, the steering position of the paddle—inert—seems best discussed here.

The concept is to turn the rear paddle into something similar to the rudder on a conventionally steered boat. This is done by trailing the paddle with the blade vertical behind the boat.

The stem of the paddle is then held by the left hand against the gunwale and the right hand goes up on the spade handle grip to control the movement—left or right— of the paddle as it acts as a rudder.

Note: this stroke, or position, is most effective when scudding across a lake before a mild breeze. It will *not* work when drifting downstream with the current of a river. This is because the canoe and the water are drifting at the same speed and there are no opposing forces working against the side of the rudder to give steerage.

Balance Stroke

Again, this isn't truly a stroke but primarily a position.

There will be many times when you will need to make

your canoe a stable platform in the water. The classic example of this is when your partner has tied into a good-sized fish and needs to play it and work it while you control the boat with your paddle.

The best way to do this—the only way in deep water—is to stick your paddle out to the side face down, slightly under the surface of the water. Then hold it rigidly against the gunwale. The flat surface of the blade held just beneath the water will restrict any sudden moves or tipping actions by the canoe and with a little practice you will be able to move the handle rapidly to stop any movement in advance.

If you are in shallow water the best method of getting stable, solid balance is to jam the end of the paddle into the bottom and grip it against the side of the canoe, making it rigid and level.

End Paddling

Some people use the end-paddle or end-sweep instead of the reach or pull. It is not more effective, and takes more work, but for those who would like to try it, the procedure is simple.

If you're in the stern, reach back and around and paddle across the stern, side to side. Unhandy, isn't it?

For bow paddlers, lean way forward and kind of sweep the paddle across the water in front of the canoe in the desired direction to make the bow move. In either case, bow or stern, it is an unbalanced condition and most certainly not worth all the publicity the move seems to create in canoeing magazine photographs.

As you get more familiar with canoeing, and your own muscles develop—sometimes painfully—you'll probably find strokes of your own. Most certainly you will refine the basic strokes to fit your own needs and that of your canoe. No two people or canoes are alike and all the movements will be slightly different.

As a final thought, it might be wise to point out that advanced canoeing projects shouldn't be rushed into. Before you take off on a two week trek into a wilderness area, do enough close work, fishing or canoeing on local lakes and rivers to develop your skills and abilities.

In that respect canoeing is like any other sport—you must work to be good at it, must train both mind and body before you take on significant challenges. You must know the boat, know yourself, know that you and the boat can meet any and all challenges that might come.

CHAPTER 5

Loading, Special Equipment, Portaging Techniques

For many years canoes were the main freight carriers for the wilderness that was central and north central America. From the northern flats of Canada down through the great midwest to the Gulf of Mexico, from the wild northwest to the Florida swamps, the canoe hauled all cargo that had to be moved on water, be it furs or trade goods, explorers or food.

And no matter the size of the load, no matter if it was a couple of furs or eight tons of them, loading was critical. For you, too, loading, also known as packing, can make or break a trip or even a day on the lake; it can ruin the whole canoeing spectrum for you, if done wrong.

There are two primary considerations involved in loading: balance and security. If either of them is incorrect or inadequate, the consequences can be anything from irritating to absolutely disastrous.

If a load is incorrectly balanced from left to right, the canoe will lean all the time. This leaning is automatically compensated for by the paddlers, who lean or shift their weight to make the boat ride level again. For short runs this is all right, since the canoe is once again level and true and moving properly. But the shifted weight, the leaning to compensate, wears on the paddlers, puts stress on the muscles in an unbalanced way. At first, perhaps, this isn't too bad. But after a few hours it can be tiring, a few more hours can turn it into exhaustion, and still a few more can cause lances of pain that dominate your back and waist and arms for the whole trip.

So balance the load with the canoe empty, that is, without the paddlers. Do it with the canoe tied to a dock but floating free and clear. Use a unitized load—a wrapped, tied, sealed load. It might not hurt to put the whole thing in a plastic garbage bag, wrapped and tied to keep it dry in case it goes over. Balance the unitized load left to right so the canoe floats true.

Also balance the load front to back. But here there is a difference depending on the number of paddlers. Balance the weight equally between you. If you are alone, work the load to the front to compensate for your weight in the rear. This will hold the bow down so you can work the canoe around in wind. Don't place the load all the way in the front, but in the front of the middle space between the seats. Then get in and see how the boat rides. Adjust the load to tune the balance as you go, keeping in mind that all heavy objects should go as low as possible to keep the center of gravity low for stability. Canned goods, for instance, should go low, dried goods on top—all inside the sealed unit, of course.

The second consideration is security. Even if it never happens, *assume* you will roll over sometime on the trip, and load for security. Tie everything into the canoe, everything loose, everything that you aren't using at the moment. If you're going fishing, as an example, tie the tacklebox, the rods into the canoe—just lash them to the thwarts. They don't have to be tied fore and aft, but some part of them should be tied in when you're not actually holding them in your hand. Your favorite rod or shotgun can go down like a brick if it's not tied to the canoe. (Note: this is where those elastic cords earn their keep. They are easy to hook and unhook, easier than tying and retying ropes.)

A last thought on loading—no matter the kind of canoe —aluminum, glass or wood-and-canvas—there will always be a little water in the bottom. Even if there is no leak, each time you move the paddle across the boat it drips a little, and this water collects in the bottom. Under the load. Many old pros keep a sponge in the low place to soak this water up, squeeze it out now and then as they go. But the load can still get damp.

Because of this, a lot of people are going back to the old fashioned floor rack. Just use a few pieces of ¼″ x 1½″ lattice from the local lumber yard to make a rack that fits the middle section of the floor of your canoe, just under the load. (See sketch.) These can be glued and nailed together. Make sure you use waterproof glue, of course. Then paint with enamel. Make your rack the right size for the center section only—don't try to make the rack go into the bow and stern. And don't attach the rack to the boat but let it just sit on the bottom. The tying down of the load will hold the rack in and there's no sense putting any unnecessary holes in the bottom of your canoe. The main idea here is to keep the load off the bottom, out of the damp, not to furnish structural strength. Bolting the rack in might also impair the flexibility of your canoe. (Note:

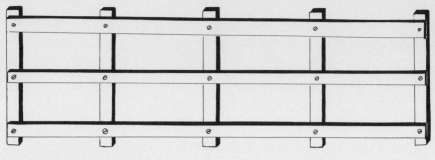

Lattice-work Rack

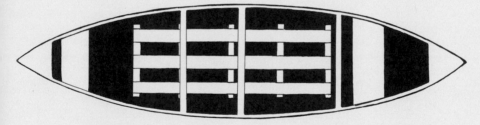

Placement of Rack in Canoe

those of you with canvas-and-wood boats needn't make the rack, as a built in rack is part of the original plan.)

Another bonus from the rack is warmth. In cold weather, late fall hunting, the bottom of a canoe is at the same temperature as the water—just above freezing. The rack keeps your feet off that cold surface, and really makes a difference.

SPECIAL EQUIPMENT

There are still other forms of specialized equipment which you might find useful—especially for long hauls, or to work back into wilderness areas.

First, a couple of drop boards on the backs of the seats can decrease tiredness dramatically. The rear seat, particularly, can be tiring after a long day of fishing because there is no back rest. If you hinge a piece of half inch plywood about seven inches wide and a foot high it can give you something to lean back against, and the difference is truly remarkable. Just put holes in the side and run a couple of pieces of rope forward to the middle thwart to hold it up. The seat can fold down to sit on when not in use. (See sketch.)

Speaking of the middle thwart—it's also known as the portaging thwart, or portaging yoke or bar. The canoe is carried with this thwart on the shoulders as a brace to hold the canoe if you're portaging alone. Portaging will be discussed shortly, but for now it's enough to note that the

Folding Seat

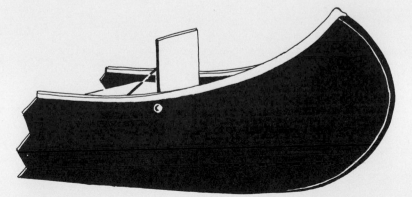

portaging bar on your canoe is most decidedly *not* designed for your shoulders. For some inane reason almost no canoe maker puts a properly shaped yoke in the middle of the canoe. Instead they throw a simple straight bar across and forget it. If you take a short portage you can just about stand it. But if you have to take even a quarter mile portage those so-called portaging bars cut you nearly in half. They're just plain murder.

But if you take a piece of one inch plywood and shape it to fit your back and shoulders, make it like a true Oriental carrying yoke, you can bolt it down on top of the middle thwart and save your back and shoulders from a lot of grief. Be sure to round and shape all edges, and then sand and varnish liberally to make it comfortable. (See illustration.)

Portaging Yoke You Can Make

There are also twin-pad commercial portaging yokes available.

Now and then a small pinch-rack on the sides can be very handy. This is a small carrier that will hold things steady without having to tie them on for safety in case you tip. Work a couple of lattice boards down with sandpaper until they're smooth, and attach them against the inside of the canoe. These are especially good for maps or sketchbooks and the like. If you drill holes all the way through the canoe wall for mounting the rack, be sure and caulk the holes liberally when you put the small bolts through. Even though they're above waterline and won't cause leaking, it doesn't hurt to keep the chance of moisture from working into the fiberglass ends, and caulking on aluminum will keep bolts from rattling or working loose.

For hunters, a gun rack is almost a must. Any commercial plastic-covered rack can be used, but be sure to have all holes above waterline, and caulk well when installing. The gun rack doubles well for bows and fishing rods, using elastic cord to lash things into place.

For any extended use, a small first aid pack mounted in the canoe is another near must. It can of course be carried in a separate pack, but the little metal kits fit so well under a seat and are so much more handy there that it's a good idea to put one in the canoe. Just mount it with small screws, using caulking, and you'll know where it is when you need it.

(Incidentally, for canoeing in southern swamps, be sure the first aid kit contains a snakebite mini-kit. They are now saying that the cut-and-suck doesn't need to be done, but take the kit anyway. If you get bitten, it's sure nice to have the option to do what you want—and besides, ideas may change again and we'll go back to old methods.)

Also, bolted up beneath the front seat, well out of the way, it's smart to put a small wooden box to carry a sealed-in-two-plastic-bags emergency survival kit. Just in case. Chances are you'll never need it, and if you're going back into wilderness you will never start out without adequate food or provisions.

But . . .

A rope could break, you could lose your cargo, you could find yourself alone in some pretty deep woods and in some pretty deep trouble. A storm could bring it all down to just you and your canoe.

If you have an emergency survival kit sealed and ready, it can give you a fantastic edge against possible danger and acute empty-belly. Every year dozens of people get stranded in wilderness areas with no food and no easy access to survival ingredients. So make up the kit in some of your free time, then you'll have it if the need arises.

Suggested items for the emergency kit are listed below. Add any personal necessary medications (insulin, etc.).

One spool of 50 pound test braided fishing line.

One small box of assorted hooks.

One small box of assorted sinkers.

One small double container of salt and pepper.

A waterproof container full of waxed matches (just dip them in paraffin).

One small bottle of aspirins.

One roll of gauze.

One roll of stretch-bandage. (This and the gauze sealed in plastic, and in addition to the normal first aid kit.)

Four emergency ration high food value candy bars, each sealed individually.

One small penknife with *very* sharp blades.

One tightly folded piece of thin plastic, six by six feet (for rain shelter).

One tube stick of mosquito and fly repellent.

One jar of petroleum jelly.

One tube of Chapstick.

One small bar of soap.

The above gives you a fair cross section of stuff which you might need in an emergency. Just make certain that the container is tightly sealed and strongly attached so it won't come loose even if badly jarred.

PORTAGING EQUIPMENT

If you head back into the woods or wilderness areas, it's a very good bet that sooner or later you're going to run out of water. Sooner or later you're going to have to pick that boat up and carry it. Sooner or later you're going to have to portage.

Whole books have been written about portaging and heaven only knows how many "cute" stories abound with titles centered around portaging (Portage Puddin', and the like). But what it all really comes down to is picking up the canoe and carrying it, and there are a few tricks which can make this tiring task a bit easier.

First, a sweatshirt or jacket rolled up for padding can save a lot of wear on your shoulders. Especially if you're working alone. And if you are alone, remain flexible. There are two basic ways to carry a canoe on portage—overhead, with your head up inside the canoe and the portaging yoke on top of your shoulders; or hanging on the side, with your shoulder caught up under the edge of the gunwale. Of the two, the overhead is probably the easiest, particularly if you have to portage a long distance—anything over a quarter mile. The overhead allows balancing of the load, an ease of carrying not provided by the side carry. But now and then vary the load over to the side to change the muscles under strain.

Two things to remember for the single portager: first, don't try to do too much. That canoe will weigh somewhere around seventy pounds, and that's enough to carry. Leave

your other gear and make two trips. Three if you must. But don't try to do it all at once because you might strain your muscles and they don't come back rapidly. A sudden strain could ruin your whole trip and make just getting home a survival trial.

Second, take it low and slow. No matter the distance of the portage, even on very short distances, stop often to rest by propping the front of the canoe up on a limb and getting out from under the weight. And then get off your feet. Take a short sit-down break every fifty yards or so if you're in brush or hills, and get away from the boat. Get on your bottom with your feet up in the air against a tree, and relax your whole body. Take these breaks often; don't push yourself. Speed portaging proves nothing and just wastes energy.

Two person portages seem in some strange way to be more than twice as easy. It's as though the extra person is really two or three more people.

Here the overhead is by far the easiest way to carry the canoe. Each person takes an end, head up in the canoe, gunwales resting on the shoulders. Padding, a shirt or jacket, on the shoulders is nice for this, but not as necessary as when portaging alone.

Again, even with two people, take many breaks and don't try to do too much. Leave your gear behind and come back for it rather than try to carry it all at once. Weight and distances can be deceptive and what seems light at the start can prove crippling halfway.

On gear left behind, make your foodstuffs safe. Just throw a rope over a limb about ten feet off the ground and pull your gear up in the air because during portaging it's wise to remember bears. They can be totally destructive.

Many camps and not a few piles of stored gear have been torn to pieces in just a few moments. It can happen so fast that you can't run to stop it. Bears take a dim view of interruptions anyway, and if one does start tearing your gear apart, let him. And if he wants your canoe, give him that, too. And if it's a sow with cubs, give her everything and get away, as rapidly as possible without running wildly. As this book was being written, three boys in Canada were killed by a bear while they were on a canoeing trip on a wilderness lake. They had been trout fishing and the bear wanted their trout and he'd attacked the boys because they stood between his belly and the fish.

Another thing that seems to happen only when you're portaging, or most when you're portaging, is the meeting of moose. If you're in moose country, which is basically the same as bear country, and you should meet a moose on the trail—not uncommon, because moose often use portaging trails to get from one lake to another—immediately surrender. Don't argue. Drop the canoe and get up the nearest tree as fast as you can. Moose are unpredictable and utterly untrustworthy. Always assume the worst, assume they'll attack, and act accordingly. Save yourself.

Understand that caution is the byword in wilderness portaging.

A last tip on portaging: the ease with which you carry something can make all the difference. You'll find, most particularly with the two man portage, that a canoe seems to lend itself admirably to being carried. Take a hint from that and pack your other gear to match the canoe. If, for instance, you pack your food in a sack it'll whip you to carry it a mile or so. But if you pack it in a good backpack, the pack is easy to carry when you portage and gives you consolidation of your gear so that it doesn't get scattered around. When you put your camping equipment in your pack just wrap it in a plastic trash bag, and then tie the pack into the canoe when you get to the water again.

SPECIAL EQUIPMENT THAT DOESN'T SEEM TO FIT ANYWHERE ELSE

Take a mask and snorkel. Those back-in lakes are usually clear and the fish unafraid. Snorkeling is a wonderful way to spend one of those muggy-hot afternoons when the sun is blazing down and the mosquitos are thirsting for your blood. The water gives a blessed relief from both heat and bugs, and the mask reveals a whole world sliding by underneath your canoe. It's also easy to sneak up on mallard hens exercising their ducklings when you've got the mask on. And seeing all those little feet squiggling down from the mirrored surface is something that will bring smiles to you for the rest of your life.

Taking canoeing trips—there's so much good that the minor bad things somehow don't stick in your mind . . .

CHAPTER 6

Reading Water and Weather

With the exception of whitewater, it isn't strictly necessary that you understand water to enjoy canoeing, unless you want to put a polish on your watercrafting. You know the boat slides along on top. And if it's a river, the current goes one way or the other. And that's about all you really need to know. With whitewater, of course, it's mandatory that you understand pile-ups and eddies—everything. There will be a chapter later on whitewater, and if you're even idly contemplating taking a wild-river trip you should read it and anything else you can find about whitewater. Rapids demand knowledge, and the price of ignorance can be nothing less than a direct danger to your life.

But right now we're concerned more with understanding, first, other kinds of waters—mild rivers, swamps, lakes—and second, the weather. These two things, the water and the weather, combine to make the backbone and skeletal structure of the watercrafting experience, and knowing them can increase your fun.

Perhaps it should be emphasized that while the information here is correct, and will help, it is not complete and can't be. Whole books have been written about the subject of understanding water; ships' captains devote their lives to water and weather and still don't know it all.

If you are seriously going into this business of water-crafting, you should find and read as many books as possible about both subjects.

MIGHTY—AND PLACID—RIVERS

At the outset, if you are considering a large river trip—down the Mississippi, the Ohio, or any other of the so-called big and placid rivers—don't start until you read Mark Twain's *Life on the Mississippi*. Aside from being a wonderful book, funny and alive and warm, there is more about reading water in that one book than you're likely to find in ten others. Samuel Clemens—Mark Twain—was an accomplished river pilot, but perhaps more important, he can tell what he knew in such a way that it sticks. And what held true of mighty rivers in the late 1800s is true today. The book can save you endless hours of problems in understanding current and snags and eddies, and entertain you in the process.

The first thing to understand in dealing with large and seemingly slow moving rivers (they aren't, really) is that you are in reality looking at two distinct rivers. Going downstream it is one river, but going upstream it is something else again—a whole different brute. And *brute* is the right word. They are most decidedly different rivers, the up and down, and should be considered as such.

Upstream, if you are considering such a trip, is a lot like war. You face formidable challenges, against the current and most often the wind, and all you have is a paddle and your back. To undertake an upstream trip on a large river is a huge job and shouldn't be contemplated unless you are in great shape. If you do decide to go, however, there are some hints which can save tremendous amounts of work.

First, stay out of the middle of the river. This is partially to avoid traffic. There are usually immense barges, container ships, sometimes freighters, using the river as a highway of commerce. Just their bow-wave can swamp you, if you're too close. But traffic is only part of the reason to avoid the middle. The most important reason is that the current is strongest on a straight stretch in the middle of a river.

And current, endless, implacable, crushing current is the enemy on an upriver trip. Anything you can do to cheat current—*anything*—is worth doing. Stay out of the middle, and then take the shortest possible route. Stay on the inside of each turn, because here, too, the current is slowest. It has to move faster to wheel around the outside of a curve, and if you go out there and try to buck it, you might find the work too much. Cut all the corners as tight as possible to the inside, and move to the very edge on the straight stretches.

Over there, on the edge, you'll find the true gold of upriver travel—the eddies. Eddies are an expression of current confusion, an indication that the current has lost its force, its drive. In some cases, the eddies are actually little currents moving in a sweeping circle *against* the main current flow of the river. So look for the little curved sweeps of water in along the edge, the twisting burbles, and paddle from one to the next: eddy jump. It's the best way to get upriver.

A note of caution: eddies tend to collect junk. Trash, old logs, snags, etc., all find their way into an eddy and hang there, circling, until they are bumped out by a bigger log, or the current changes and releases them. Care should be exercised to avoid hull damage from hitting them.

Stay on the inside of the curves, work the eddies as much as possible, stay out of the middle—all of these will help a little. And luckily, the wind—the second enemy—conforms very closely to the water. It usually seems to go in the same direction, and acts in most ways just like the current: strongest in the middle and outsides of curves, "eddies" along the tight side. So if you cheat the water, you cheat the wind.

The primary thing to remember about upriver trips is that if you stop, even for a moment, if you quit paddling just to take a breather, the current, and usually the wind, will drive you back. You must paddle all the time, constantly, or you lose ground. So take a long, thin rope along, and if you wish to rest, pull in to the side and tie up to a branch. It's a crushing thing to keep slipping back all the time.

Downriver trips are just the opposite, obviously. Hit the middle, take the outside of curves, don't work the eddies. But there are some things to keep in mind. There is a temptation, for instance, to pull a Huck Finn and just let it all go loose—float down the river in the lazy sun with a line over the side, snoozing off and on, making up in this one trip for all the pressure that life will ever dump on you. And it *is* a wonderful way to relax. But remember the barges. Some of those river giants take two or three miles to turn, and if they come around a corner and you're sleeping right under their bow, even if they see you they won't be able to turn in time. So keep an eye open.

The other thing to remember about downriver trips is that you won't be able to steer unless you paddle. You can turn the boat with end-sweeps or reaching strokes, but the boat won't steer unless you're going faster than the water, or paddling downstream.

Some final notes about long, big river trips. Take good water in plastic jugs. Don't drink river water even if it's boiled. Twain did, but modern pollutants don't boil out, and it simply isn't safe.

Snags—buried or half buried underwater logs and rocks—can dump you on a downriver trip. Keep an eye out for them. A snag close to the surface will cause the water to bulge upward in warning.

You can also encounter heavy fog on the big rivers. If you see it coming, get to shore and wait it out. Don't, under any circumstances, try to keep going. If you get caught by fog, watch the current—then go across-current, paddling steadily and as straight as you can, until you reach the nearest shore, and then wait it out.

Two things to bear in mind about camping next to the river on long trips: First, keep the canoe handy and ready to go at all times. Depth can vary wildly in a matter of minutes if they decide to open the gates on a dam spillway upstream. You can find your campsite suddenly under water, so be ready.

Second, air moves away from water in the afternoon, but moves toward the water at night (assuming now that there is no wind). When the air comes back at night, it brings a faint chill. So you might want to camp with the future movement of air in mind and keep shelter between you and the chill.

Finally, remember that the big rivers are really crowded

—not just with other traffic, but with dams and lock systems. Don't try to travel at night unless it's an emergency, and then stick to the sides, and go slowly.

SMALL RIVERS, SLOW

Placid, uncrowded, small rivers are the classic fun canoeing trip. Here all the same basic rules apply as to water reading—upriver, stay inside, work eddies, etc.; downriver, go the middle for speed—but without the big river hassles. There is seldom fog, usually not too much wind, and the traffic is limited to the odd crazy speedboat or other canoeists. While there are dams and breakwaters to hold the current in channels, they are not as common on small rivers and more easily handled and gotten around with minimal portaging.

Camping rules still apply. Night air moves toward the water, bringing chill; day air moves away. If you fish for catfish, common on both small and large placid, muddy rivers—and they are truly delicious when fried in cornmeal until the meat flakes with a fork—you might try an overnight line. Have the sinker about a foot above a medium size hook. Use worms, and leave the hook on the bottom, under an overhanging tree in an eddy and go to bed. You'll probably get one for breakfast.

A caution on small, placid rivers. There is a possibility in early spring of significant sudden flooding—flash-flooding. This can also come from heavy rains upriver. Flash floods do not behave as so many films insist on showing them. A wall of water does *not* come roaring down on you suddenly out of nowhere, crushing you and carrying you off. What *can* happen is that the water level rises very

Canoe as tent pole—when you're out of range of rising waters

fast, so fast that you haven't time to break camp or spend many minutes packing your gear. For this reason, it's a good idea in the spring, when there is snow- or ice-melt upriver, or if it's been raining a lot upriver, to make a hasty-camp: one which can be broken easily and rapidly, with the canoe already *tied* in the water and loaded with everything but your sleeping gear. Then if the water comes up fast you're all set to leave fast.

SMALL RIVERS, FAST AND SHALLOW

Exploring small rivers—large creeks—seems to have been designed specifically for the canoe, especially the twelve to sixteen footer with a shallow keel. You become an active part of the water, skimming along under overhanging tree limbs, winding through the country.

But those same creeks can gut your boat if you're not ready for them. In a very real way they're more hazardous than known rough water or wild whitewater, because somehow you don't expect a creek or little river to rebel. Yet they do, and probably the most important things to watch out for in small rivers are the quick shoals, the shallows that surprise which can be just around the next tight bend. They can come so fast that you only have time to react once, and that's it.

As with any hazard, the best defense is awareness. If you are working with two people, the bow person should not bother to paddle but take full responsibility for watching ahead. The canoe doesn't pull much water—sit too deep—but spots which are too shallow even for the canoe will appear as upward bulges in the water out ahead. The bow paddler should at first use a claw or reach stroke to pull the bow away, warning the stern paddler at the same time; and then, if there isn't time to turn completely away, should use the paddle to fend off the rock or snag. The end of the paddle might get chewed up a bit, but it's better than tearing the bottom of the canoe out.

If the spot coming is too shallow for the canoe, as in a gravel bed in a stream, the bow person should jump out and stop the canoe. This is done by putting both hands on the gunwales (one on either side to balance properly) and vaulting into the water. It must be done fast, as fast as possible, or the boat will be on the shoals and the bottom abraded. Of course, repairs can be made, but it's best to avoid the need for them in the first place.

In particularly tight creeks, where the corners come fast and sharp, teamwork can make a lot of difference. Be sure that you both know how the other works. If the bow paddler claw-reaches to the right while the stern paddler claw-reaches to the left, for example, it can cut the speed of the turn in half.

If you are exploring these fast, small rivers alone, all responsibility falls on you. Take station slightly ahead of the rear seat, or just back of the middle, to even the weight and get the canoe floating straight and level. With all the weight in the stern the bow is raised, which can obstruct vision a bit, but it lowers the stern so that the canoe takes more water clearance than is normal.

Watch for upward bulges, or ripple-riffle places that mean shallow water—really *watch*. All the time. They come so fast and there is such a short time to react!

When alone, the best method of averting a problem is to reach over the side with your shoulder weight and jam the paddle down into the bottom, *hard*, and swing on it like a peg in the ground. This will stop the canoe and give you time to think of a way out or around the problem. Don't be afraid to get out of the canoe and wade, pulling the boat around the bad places.

SHALLOW LAKES, SWAMPS, SLOUGHS

Perhaps the one true advantage of a canoe over other boats is that it allows you access to very shallow water. This lets you in where big bass and lily-pad pike are hiding, where duck hunting is best, where wild rice grows and can be harvested.

And actually, there are very few problems to be encountered in shallow lake or slough exploration. The water is too shallow to allow big waves, there is no current to drive you into rocks; there are usually no rocks anyway. It's all a smooth shot, over tame water, and the only thing which can really slow you down or bother you is weeds and lily-pads. Incidentally, if you have an old canoe—no matter the composition—you'll feel that those weeds seem to almost grab the surface. If you wax the bottom with carwax to fill the scrapes and scratches, you'll find that that canoe will pull through a bit easier. Not a lot, but enough to make it worth doing.

The main problem you will encounter is that same old hassle of mosquitos. Bugs abound in shallow tame waters, so be certain you have your repellent with you.

Shallow waters also suggest another form of locomotion: poling. For wild-ricing or duck hunting, using a pole instead of paddling is probably the better way to go. It allows more control, because you can jam that long pole down into the mud bottom and hold the boat right there, whereas the paddle isn't really long enough.

The problem with poling is that it's necessary to stand up. And all those cliché jokes about standing up in a canoe are true. It's so easy to tip that it's frightening—the thing just flips. So be prepared to get wet a few times until you get your hand-eye-foot-pole coordination down pat.

You can get the pole from a lumber yard. Get a three-inch diameter pine pole, ten feet long. Sand and varnish, repeating until it's "tight" and smooth and will keep the water out of the wood. The ends are left flat. They make fancy forked gizzies to put on the ends to keep them out of the mud, and they help a little, but you don't need them at first.

Position yourself by standing in the middle of the canoe, feet apart, balanced, and put the pole down over the side into the bottom mud or the weeds. Then push backwards, running your hands up the pole until you are nearly out of wood. Now pull the pole out—a process which usually puts you close to tipping or left hanging on the pole—and put it slightly ahead of center, on the bottom again, and repeat the process. Poling is good for getting through very thick weeds, but that's about it, really.

A possible hazard in swamps and shallow lakes is submerged logs. They float even with the surface, and in the stillness of a weedy back lagoon they're just impossible to see. If the bow of the canoe should run up on one, it probably won't hurt the bottom much, but it will destroy the balance of the canoe by lifting it partially out of the water. This in turn can tip the canoe, and if you happen to be wild-ricing and dump your harvest, it can be frustrating.

There are two warning signs of submerged logs. The first is small bumps that stick up out of the water. (This can be a little confusing because what you are looking for closely resembles a mud-turtle's head.) Watch for a sharpish little wood-tip sticking up off one of the knots of the log—the knot bumps float a little higher. After a time it's fairly easy to tell the knot from a turtle's head— the head will be slightly more pointed and moving a little with the water. But at first it can be a bit difficult, so go easy.

(NOTE: for those who have never harvested wild rice and don't know how, the procedure is very simple. Take your canoe and a couple of flails—just sticks about an inch in diameter and two feet long—and head for the nearest rice lake—in season, of course. It will probably be late August or early September. The season varies considerably, depending on where you are. There are also usually complicated, stringent laws giving Indians the first run through, so be sure and check your local state office first.

Actual harvesting is easy. You just glide into the rice along the side of the lake, bend the ripened heads over the side of the canoe, and beat them with the sticks until all the rice grains fall into the canoe. The rice is especially delicious when cooked as stuffing in a wild duck or grouse. Or the rice can be sold.)

LARGE LAKE; STORM SITUATIONS

A flat statement of warning: unless it is absolutely imperative—an emergency situation—no truly large lake should ever be crossed in a canoe or any other small, thin boat. It is simply not safe, under any condition, and the chances of a life-endangering situation developing are so favorable that it just shouldn't be done. Ever.

If you find yourself facing such a crossing, in which you will have to go out a couple of miles, find some way instead to go around the edge, staying close to shore. When you are limited to hand/arm power, your speed is minimal. A storm can blow up while you are out there, a storm which didn't show before you left, and the consequences can be tragic. Flotation, good life vest, excellent physical condition and swimming ability—none of these things mean anything if the waves are high enough to keep your head under water. And such waves can be common on a large lake in high wind.

In fact the only true hazard on a large lake, the only thing that requires "reading" the water is high wind.

Everything else is the same as on a small lake: snags show at the surface as little points; floating logs will be a sudden, hard line in the normally soft line of the water.

But high wind—that has a signature all its own. As you progress along the side of the lake watch and *feel* out towards the middle. If high wind is affecting some other part of the lake out of sight there will be a surge in the water, a kind of movement beneath the waves that somehow you can sense. It is very hard to describe other than to say it is a sensation that you will *know* when it happens: an unmistakable gut-feeling.

Visually, high wind will present a flattening appearance to the water horizon—a hiss-cut way out where the water meets the sky. If this wind is truly vicious, say seventy to ninety or so knots, it will literally slice the tops off the waves.

In a gale you should not be out on a lake, but this kind of wind can come up out of nowhere, covering an area as much as a quarter of a mile across, and you should get out of the water and onto land as quickly as possible. Don't even try going around the edge. Canoes at best are not too stable, and in high waves or gale winds they lose even that minimal stability.

If, for some insane reason, you *must* be on a big lake in high waves, there are several things which have to be done for safety. First, tie yourself in some way to the canoe—just .a rope around your waist to the middle thwart (here's the rope again, always needed). If you get dumped, even with a life vest on, the canoe is the only refuge.

Should need dictate that you run against the wind and waves, take them bow-on, either slightly left or right, but preferably head on. You will be subjected to violent slamming, and be soaked, but there is a chance you'll make it.

If you have to run with the waves and wind, take it straight down. Get into the middle or slightly forward of middle, to raise the stern to meet the waves, and ride straight down the waves. You probably won't make it in either case, with or against, but these are the best—the safest—ways to try.

When/if dumped on a large lake in high waves the struggle for air is the whole fight. *Don't* leave the canoe. Hang on, if you aren't tied, to a thwart on the down-wave side of the canoe and breathe every time you get a chance. You will be taking waves over your head often, so learn to breathe in snatches—take gulps of air whenever your head is clear. The wind-waves will carry you into some shore and the primary aim should be to maintain life until that shore comes.

WEATHER KNOWLEDGE

To be truly understanding of the weather you might expect on a long canoeing trip, or on a day-long shot, it's necessary to study the weather all year.

Start by making your own rough weather graph during the winter, when you're facing down time from boating anyway. Watch the weather maps and satellite pictures on television and catalog every rough front that comes through by date and time, and keep track of how long it stays and what it does.

Usually you'll find that the fronts come out of the northwest, seem to cycle through every week to ten days, and tend to drop some moisture—the amount depending on region—before they move on. After each front cycles through, there will be a period of either clear weather, or partly cloudy weather, at first cool and then slightly warmer, and then a couple or three very nice days—and then the next front.

There are, of course, exceptions. Some weird storms come, freak blasters out of nowhere, that haven't been predicted and don't fall into any rule pattern. But most often the fronts can be predicted, and if you spend some time keeping track of them, you'll find it much easier to plan your next trip.

Also, don't be afraid to use the experts. Give the local meteorology office or the television weather forecaster a call before you leave and check things out. They can help out a great deal, despite the way most of us laugh at them. Use all information at your disposal, and then take a good poncho and you're covered.

In the field—on the lake or river—you're pretty much committed to whatever weather comes: a paddle doesn't give you enough speed to outrun a storm. Still, keep a weather eye out, most particularly if you are on the edge of a large body of water, or in an area where lightning is a problem.

Treat *any* buildup of clouds with a cautious, wary eye. If they're little and white and fluffy they might be "scout" clouds: clouds which come before a major front. Watch them. If they change to all gray, a ceiling, head for shore before the weather develops further.

Massive, black, boiling thunderheads will kill you. Get off the lake before they even begin to get close. Any high, dark cloud structure which might generate lightning is extremely bad to face. Many people each year are struck by lightning while boating, and it's a bad way to go because it's so unnecessary. Just get off the lake when the clouds build. Cut yourself a little slack and wait until it's over—bank-fish for awhile.

You didn't get into canoeing to hurry.

CHAPTER 7

Kayaks

In a strange kind of way, a reversal of roles has occurred in pleasure boating that at one time would have seemed impossible, or at least highly unlikely.

Boats originally designed purely for work, for their ability to perform specialized tasks, have come completely around to being designed totally for pleasure.

Canoes were conceived initially as work boats to make all the water highways available to Indians, and later to early settlers, trappers, explorers. And the canoe did well at it, and still slicks along those highways with ease. Yet the modern canoe is designed more with pleasure in mind than with any kind of work.

And with the kayak—the thoroughbred of watercrafting—this reversal of roles is even more pronounced.

Sleek, marvelously fast, as graceful and quick as a ballet dancer, the kayak is such a wonder of beauty and speed that many people can't believe it the first time. It's as if you're wearing the boat, wearing another skin that kisses the water and allows you freedom in an element heretofore denied human beings. The kayak is probably the most directly joyful boat it's possible to use for watercrafting. The canoe or raft is a vehicle to get somewhere, to do something; to fish, or view country, to explore. With the kayak the boat is everything. It's an art form in itself, a kind of dancing with the water; just using the kayak is the whole kayaking experience.

And yet the kayak was designed as a kind of weapon. Perfected by the Eskimo, the kayak was used as an extension of the hunting weaponry of this far northern hunter. Its light wood frame, graceful and tied with leather thongs, was covered with a watertight skin sheath, usually of sealskin. The Eskimo strapped himself in, tied a kind of apron around himself underneath his armpits, and used a two-bladed paddle to skim in pursuit of seals, walrus, small whales. Harpoons were tied on top of the kayak, lashed with floats made of other skins. With this needle-boat he could get in close, drive a harpoon in, and rapidly get out of the way. Many giant animals were taken by this almost prehistoric, and highly successful, boat-man combination. To use a skin boat and flimsy harpoon to take a four ton walrus whose tusk could slice open the boat—the kayak *had* to be good.

And now, modern kayaks, made of synthetics, ribless, with paper-thin shells, light beyond belief, are challenging, and whipping, the wildest whitewater of the wild western rivers. Today's kayaks are being designed purely for pleasure, for the thrill of proving the ability of the watercrafter.

"It's like turning into a waterbug," one new kayaker said. "A kind of skimmer that doesn't even break the surface of the water. I just sat on top and *moved!*"

It is a truly rewarding experience, and will give you as much as you want to take out of it. A flick of the arms can move you across a river or pond, a minimal amount of work can skim you miles. The kayak really is a wonder, and if you're considering getting involved in kayaking, it's a sure bet that you're going to love it.

But as with anything, the amount of knowledge you have can greatly increase your enjoyment. And with kayaks, which are getting more and more specialized and tightly classed, which are rapidly emerging as a sport-form—and which tip just about as fast as they move—with kayaks, knowledge can be critical.

And the first thing you have to know is yourself.

If you are an already avid kayaker, some of this is going to sound pretty simple to you. But for those who are just starting, it's necessary to examine closely just what you wish to do with your kayak. If, for instance, you are going into the competitive aspect of kayaking—racing or doing the slalom, rallying—the kind of kayak you choose, the amount of money you can spend on it, can greatly influence your success. If you are getting a kayak for a hobby, or something new to do, but aren't going to turn into a purist, it's possible to save tremendous amounts of money and still get what you want. The problem is being specific enough to make a decision.

It's nearly impossible to even name the many kinds of kayaks. There are masses of them—cross-listed, overlapping, unclassifiable. Some people break them into two groups: slalom and downriver, and perhaps for the moment we ought to stick with that. More precise definitions can come a little later.

DOWNRIVER KAYAKS

The downriver—also called wildwater—kayaks are designed for one thing: straight-ahead speed. The keel line is purely straight. If you view the keel from the front, you can't miss the pronounced V-shape of the hull, especially on the older models. Imagine how this V-shape cuts straight ahead through the water. The hulls on some newer models are slightly rounded, but they are still narrow, still have the same effect. This downriver boat isn't much for turning and is every bit as tippy as it looks, at least until you pick up a little speed. Then it seems to stabilize a bit, but only a bit—sort of like a bicycle: the slower it moves the harder it is to balance.

SLALOM KAYAKS

The slalom kayaks are designed more for turning. Look at the side: there will probably be a pronounced rocker, up at stern and bow, for quick turning. Again, go up front and look back along the keel, or where the keel is supposed to be. There will be practically no keel on a slalom boat. Note the flat bottom; or maybe, up by the bow, there might be just the hint of a V-shape to give a touch more tracking ability. For the person new to kayaking, this flat bottom seems to give the craft a mind of its own, a will directed to turning sideways no matter what. But once mastered, the flat bottom makes the boat a quick, maneuverable thing, a delight to its pilot in waters that would chew a more conventional canoe or kayak to pieces.

So, for making a decision initially, it depends on what you wish to do. For flatwater speed and tracking, the deep

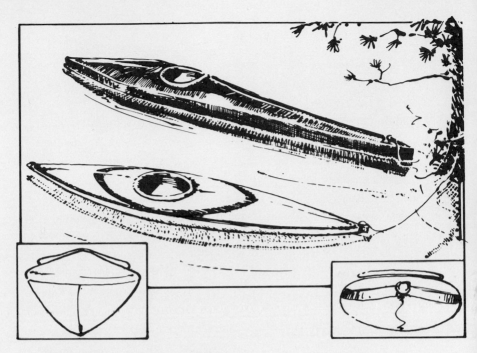

Slalom Kayak (bottom and left)
Downriver Kayak (upper and right)

V is what you want. For rapids, whitewater, you want the shallow keel—the slalom boat.

OTHER KAYAKS

But there are still other facets to take into account before making a decision. The slalom and downriver kayaks are usually one-person jobs designed for racing in running water. But there are many other kinds of kayaks. In between the slalom and downriver models you'll find recreational kayaks with a mixture of features. There are one, two, even four-person kayaks—usually built of molded plywood, sometimes with rudders for easy steering. Complicating things still further are the closed deck canoes—one- and two-person craft which look much like a kayak, but which take a single bladed paddle and a kneeling, not sitting, paddler. There are also the single-person surfing kayaks which look like bent sticks of chewing gum (design still being perfected)—bluntnosed, bluntsterned, bow and stern radically upswept.

You can, obviously, do any of the above variations on the kayak, or canoe, and just as obviously, a book covering all the variations would take several volumes. We will have to content ourselves with only the most popular versions, those sanctioned by the International Canoe Federation for racing or rally competition. They are also the most popular by far, so it's likely that your specific kayak needs will be covered.

Before getting down to uses and cases, because we're dealing with a kind of thoroughbred boat, it's necessary to define things in a technical way: in other words, use some numbers.

To meet ICF regulations, the downriver kayak is limited to a length of 14 feet, 8 inches, and has to be at least 23¾ inches wide. Longer and narrower might be a little faster, but won't meet racing specs.

Likewise, the slalom kayak has to be at least 13 feet, 2 inches long and the same 23¾ inches wide. These specs help to emphasize paddling ability over design, though working within these limits, there's still a lot of room for design differences.

Besides numbers another technical phrase you're likely to hear relates to *volume*. Volume is the room inside a kayak. If the kayak were filled with water, a high-volume kayak would hold more than a low-volume. A low-volume kayak is trickier to handle, less stable. It demands more skill. Once mastered, however, a low-volume job is quicker on the turns and is good on up to moderately rough water. But really rough water takes a high-volume kayak. So do large people—and so do trips, when you need the room for storage of equipment and food.

Once you've made your decision, actually acquiring a kayak differs drastically from acquiring a canoe. With the canoe you could do everything from finding a clunker to building from a kit—they all served. Considering the tricky ways of the kayak, it doesn't pay to get loose. Buy a kayak, either new or used, from a reputable source and stay away from quickie-kits or seemingly super deals. Later, when you're expert, you may want to buy a kit, and there are several on the market, but don't do it initially. And when you do get the kit, if you do, follow instructions carefully and get help from somebody who knows synthetics well and will assist you.

A final note before getting into the boat itself. If your heart is set on competition, there are things to be said for avoiding the "beginners" boats and going for the hard-to-handle model you'll ultimately wind up using. At first it will take extra work to master, but you'll avoid the expense of two craft and the effort of having to learn a portion of your techniques all over again.

CRAFT CONSTRUCTION

Having decided, first, to get into kayaking and, second, the kind of kayaking to get into, it is time to take a closer look at the craft itself.

Both slalom and wildwater kayaks have similar parts.

The hull is a single, molded piece of synthetic material—fiberglass, Kevlar, polyester. And though we've talked about keel lines, there is no true keel as such, only the line, deep or shallow.

The deck is also a single, molded piece of synthetic material. It covers the hull, keeps the water out and is more or less rounded so the water rolls off. Because the deck takes less punishment than the hull, it is usually constructed less ruggedly; this also keeps the weight down.

Somewhere near the center of the deck is the cockpit hole, and fore and aft in the deck may be a couple of pencil-size holes for grabloops: pieces of rope handy for retrieving a loose kayak.

Fitting down into the cockpit hole is the third molded piece of the kayak, a unit made up of a small seat, the coaming (also called the cockpit rim), and the hipbraces. The hipbraces will grab you, but without putting your legs to sleep. The coaming resembles big lips which hold you like a cigarette—or a flange, as if you were sitting inside the bell of a tuba. The coaming is raised up sufficiently from the deck of the kayak so that you can fit the bottom elastic edge of the spray skirt in between the coaming lip and the deck.

The spray skirt? A special piece of kayaking equipment: a high-waisted skirt that keeps the water out of your lap and keeps the kayak more or less watertight when you're doing the Eskimo roll. It's the seal between you and the kayak, a kind of puckered washer. The bottom edge of the spray skirt ties in between the coaming and the deck. It should fit loosely enough so that it comes off easily when you want to get away in a hurry. It comes with a release cord for tugging the skirt loose quickly at just those moments. Needless to say, the release cord should be in front of you and visible after you've slipped the bottom edge of the skirt over the coaming.

In a sense, the kayaker *wears* the kayak, buttocks wedged into the seat, knees wedged against padded knee-braces, the feet firmly planted against some sort of foot-brace, usually simply a wooden rod across the inside. Leg pressure to the side pretty much locks a person into the seat, though *lock* might be too strong a word. It does make a newcomer to the sport wonder how to go about getting out of the boat if needed in an emergency.

No problem. Simply relax foot and knee pressure, tug the quick-release spray skirt off the coaming, and gravity will pull you out and down. To speed your exit still more, you can put both hands on the deck near your waist and give a shove. Most people say it's impossible to get trapped inside an overturned kayak, but it's nice to know for yourself for sure. Eventually the idea will be to stay inside, to do the Eskimo roll, to right an overturned kayak without leaving the seat. But that comes later.

One more necessary item for your kayak. Many kayaks won't float on their own when swamped. They do not have the built in flotation chambers of canoes. So vinyl flotation bags are cheap insurance. You need one forward of the footbrace and one aft of the cockpit. Old inner tubes have been substituted for the fitted bags to save money, but they have also been known to float loose in a pinch. Flotation bags don't cost much; you can blow up the fitted ones prior to launching and deflate them for storage, and they don't add much weight. It's not a good place to skimp.

And speaking of skimping: another lousy place to cut expenses is safety gear. A person can find deals, and cut corners, and save a few dollars. But if you're going where you'll need a helmet, get one. And don't take a football helmet and call it good enough. The helmet needs holes in the top: when you're fighting a current upside down in the water, the last thing you need is a helmet full of water.

Use the same life vest and safety rules as covered in the canoeing section—good, *safe*, approved-by-the-Coast-Guard equipment.

And if you anticipate kayaking on mountain rivers in the spring, you might get a wetsuit, or at least a wetsuit top to keep you warm when you roll over.

PADDLES

First, look at one of the double-bladed kayaking paddles. The blades are almost always "feathered," at right angles to each other. When one blade is submerged on the power stroke, the other slices through the air and doesn't catch the wind. Some paddles with unfeathered blades are made, but most people avoid them because they're unnecessarily tiring to use.

As for composition, the basic wood kayak paddle you'll find in stores is all right, if often a little expensive. To cut costs a bit, look at the ones with fiberglass blades. And to economize still further, look for one of the paddle kits available.

Some of the commercial paddles are built to come apart in the middle of the shaft, and are held together, when assembled, by a metal sleeve and a screw. However, the joint is a weak point, a disadvantage. But they store well, both at home and on the river.

As to the type of paddle for you, it depends again on a

number of things. First, what kind of kayaking are you going to be doing? Square-tipped blades are preferred for slalom work where paddles tend to be more rugged and shorter than for downriver or wildwater and touring. The shape of the downriver blade is oval and asymmetrical.

Length varies roughly between 80 and 90 inches, shorter people preferring shorter paddles—although to a certain degree, paddle lengths are largely a matter of personal taste.

And finally, when the power or business face of the paddle is curved—as many people prefer it to be—you will want to know if the paddle is for right-handers or left-handers.

Really. It's not a joke.

Though a right-hander tends to prefer the right-handed paddle, and the left-hander the left, anyone can adapt to either—if need be. But why adapt? Learn to tell the difference. There *is* a difference, and you can tell it by holding the paddle in both hands with the power-face of the right blade facing the rear. If the opposite power-face is facing the sky, then you're holding a right-handed paddle. If the face does not turn to the sky, it's a left-hander.

The difference comes into play when the paddle is being used. With the right-handed paddle the right hand grips the shaft—and keeps gripping. The left hand relaxes at certain times during the stroke to let the shaft twist loosely inside the palm. With the left-handed paddle, the left hand keeps gripping.

If all this seems a little confusing or tricky just wait until you get into your kayak for the first time.

CHAPTER 8

Kayaking; Getting Wet

So the kayak is sitting there, you've got it home. Sleek, needle-pointed, it just begs to be given life on the nearest water. It is time, you think, for the maiden voyage.

And in a way it is—but first there are some fitting things to do to make certain the kayak is tuned to *your* body and mind. You've probably already tried the boat on for size, found that it seems very tight. Good. If it doesn't, something is wrong—it's too loose. Try moving the footbrace closer to you, and make certain the knee and hipbraces hold you closely. Now the spray-skirt. Tightness is *not* good in the spray-skirt. Make sure it is snug, but loose enough so it won't slow you down if you have to make an exit underwater.

Do all this fitting on a soft lawn with tight, deep grass, to avoid damaging the hull, and get in and out of the boat with great care.

A few more words of help. Too many kayakers lose their investment at this point, the point where patience is likely to pay the most: learning to control the kayak. Most kayaks are tricky things. A person can be totally familiar with water, have paddled a canoe for years, run dozens of

rapids in a raft and still not be ready to just step into a kayak and take off. The nature of a kayak, its agility, demands that its pilot be in complete control, or the kayak takes control itself, often dumping the pilot in the process. So take it easy at first. Select calm waters; a swimming pool isn't out of the question. Have a coach available, or, at the very least, a friend to help and to smooth your psyche the first time you wet-exit. Whether you use a slow moving river, or a pool, ensure a good stretch of water at least three feet deep. A cracked head during a wet-exit is no special thrill, either.

Now, there's the water, and the kayak, and the paddle, and you. Just how *do* you get into one of the darn things?

With the canoe you grab the gunwales and step into the middle. Entering a kayak is an entirely different—and more difficult—matter.

First get the kayak to the side of the water. Put the paddle from the shore or poolside out across the kayak, just to the rear of the coaming, with the flat side down on the ground. This will help balance when you get in. Now crouch, gripping the paddle bar and the coaming behind you, and put your foot into the center of the cockpit, just forward of the seat. Now bring your other foot in, then swing your bottom gently down and into the seat; pushing your legs forward at the same time, maintaining balance with the paddle to shore.

Now relax. Don't move; sort of will all your weight down in the middle, just relax and don't try to make the free-floating kayak sit in any special way. You'll note that it seeks a balance of its own, wobbly, to be sure, but a kind of central balance is found and it is at least a little stable.

Next comes the spray-skirt. Even though you aren't ready for the Eskimo roll or any rough water just yet, fit the spray-skirt. When you get in, make sure it's rolled up so you don't sit on it. When you're in, bring it down and attach it to the coaming: back first, front second and sides third.

Again relax, holding the paddle across in front of you, and let the kayak seek its own balance. It's best this first time to avoid the temptation to just go zooming off and do your own thing, even with that sleek boat seemingly quivering to go. (Kayaks actually do seem to tremble the first time.) Several maneuvers are worth practising before much else is attempted. They build confidence, show what the boat will do, give you a feel for your own abilities and limitations, and help avoid unnecessary surprises.

Getting Into Kayak

Spray Skirt

WET-EXIT

Getting out of the kayak in an upside down condition is the first maneuver to learn. It can, obviously, be a matter of survival and it should be done many times before going any further.

Roll the boat to the capsize point slowly, so you'll know where and when it comes, and go on over. As soon as it tips, release the spray-skirt and slide free. Do this a few times until you're used to it and familiar with the water.

Now it's necessary to simulate the actual conditions of a wet-exit. In fast water you want that kayak downstream of you, so it won't come down and bump your head. But you also want to hang on to the boat and paddle so they won't get away. So do several wet-exits without losing the boat or the paddle, hanging on to them as you break water upstream of the boat. Do this ten or fifteen times, until the whole maneuver is thoroughly familiar to you. If you think this faintly silly, remember you want it all automatic, so when it happens in wildwater—not if, but *when*—you will react correctly.

While working on the wet-exit it's a good idea to establish your balance points. Go to the capsize points and then, using hip motion and body movement and the paddle against the water, bring the boat back to stability. Keep working at this between wet-exit rehearsals, until the balance points are as known and automatic as the wet-exit maneuver.

A last thought about wet-exits: it's likely the boat will get swamped, filled with water, while you're practising. It's no big thing, but don't try to lift the kayak onto shore while it's still full. It's not only hard on your back, with water weighing eight pounds a gallon, but can crack the hull. Keep the boat upside down in the water and run one end up on shore to let the water run out of the cockpit before turning it over.

If anything bugs you, if *anything* doesn't work right or you are afraid or confused or a little rattled, stay with this maneuver until it's smooth. Getting out of the kayak fast and easily is obviously critical, and you must know how before you move on to any other step.

ESKIMO ROLL

The pros make it look so easy, just a snap and a flip and you've rolled over and righted yourself. But the first time you try to bring the capsized kayak back up to the top do it with a friend or coach and *only* if you absolutely know the wet-exit.

Second, before starting, it doesn't hurt to wear a face-mask to keep the water from attacking your sinuses when you hang upside down and so you can see what's happening.

The idea is to develop the beginnings of the Eskimo roll, before getting into any refinements. Get a feel for the hip action necessary to right the boat and get a feel for the way your legs, feet and hips have to lock inside for everything to come up all right.

Have your friend hold the paddle, firmly, at water level and parallel to the boat. You're going to use it the way a ballet dancer uses the bar on a wall, for support and balance.

Grab the paddle shaft with both hands, and hanging onto the shaft, tilt the boat over until you are under the water, as you would be if the boat capsized.

Now push down on the shaft, while snapping your hips to bring the kayak rolling back up. At first you will have to rely heavily on the shaft of the paddle, and your friend. But keep working at it. Work at keeping your head under water longer and longer. The longer you can keep your head down while you snap the kayak up the easier the roll will go. Also work at putting less and less pressure on the paddle shaft, using your hips and the snap more and more, until just the paddle on the surface of the water is enough.

The Eskimo Roll

That's the Eskimo roll. At first it will go rough, and you might have to wet-exit a few times, but keep at it until you can flip the kayak up with ease. Do this in calm water, with the friend still there. Keep at it until you think you know it so well you'll never have trouble with it. Then do it some more.

You can't be too good at it. Stay with both the wet-exit and the Eskimo roll until they're automatic, a normal function of your body when you're in the kayak. It's vital.

PADDLING KAYAKS

The one thing about kayak paddling is that it always sounds enormously more complicated than it really is. As a matter of fact the double-bladed paddle simplifies the complexities which the canoeist faces. The kayaker isn't plagued, for instance, with uneven pressure on one side throwing the craft off course. The double-bladed paddle works both sides of the craft at once so it holds a course.

The kayaker and the paddle are more intimately related than the canoeist and the canoe paddle. While the point of canoeing has a lot to do with exploring scenery, the point of kayaking is paddling, to a great degree. A series of precise actions, each action neatly appropriate to its own moment, that's kayak paddling.

But the search for paddling precision, while fascinating in process and result, is often a little dull in the telling. Involved, long-winded descriptions of precise moves tend to be counterproductive. And the point here is that while we're going to discuss all the moves, or most of them, and use some of the jargon, don't use it as the final, end-all of your knowledge. Use the written material, perhaps an informal coaching session with somebody who is really good, then *work* at the various strokes—and go back and forth between reading and working until it all comes together.

Skim through the following, and don't be put off by strange names; most of the time the unusual name describes a simple movement with a simple purpose.

Sweeps and Draws

These, the first two, are the basic kayaking strokes. The sweep is the ordinary turn stroke, the stroke one associates with kayaking.

Start with your back straight, the paddle held across the boat in front of you, your arms about two feet apart in the middle (or wherever is comfortable). Good posture is important here. Now lean forward, and with the blade just beneath the surface of the water, sweep it back on the side. As soon as you have finished this side, dip the other side and sweep back along that. The boat will nearly dart forward. As you can guess this is also a good stroke for turning because it pushes the boat around as you make the sweep.

The draw stroke is similar to the reaching stroke in the canoe. With the paddle straight up and down like a tree and the power-face toward you—the face in the water—reach way out to the side. Now pull back, straight towards yourself, which will draw the kayak towards the paddle.

All very simple. If you're a beginner, however, you'll probably be a bit timid about doing the sweep. Don't be. Remember that the sweep stroke is a bold and brazen thing, the turn-stroke of kayaking, so put your heart in it.

Forward Stroke

Nothing mysterious here. This stroke does just what the name states: gives you maximum push forward with minimal turn or wasted energy.

Remember what was said about the way you use a right- or left-handed paddle. If you're right-handed, the right hand is the gripping hand. Left is just the opposite.

To begin the forward stroke lean forward. Again, good posture matters. Head up, eyes front, back a straight rod of power. Insert the paddle more or less straight up and down, alongside the kayak, and pull back. As you pull back, keep the shaft of the paddle in close to the hull.

Then switch over to the other side and do the same thing. In this stroke, the common beginner's mistake is depending solely on the lower arm for the power of the stroke. Keep in mind the leverage you have with the upper arm and take advantage of it—push! Levering with that upper arm tends to even out exertion so that the whole body gets into the act. Concentrate on the leverage and the grip—not too hard, but constant in the one hand—and keep the shaft in close to the kayak. Deliver that power straight ahead for speed and control.

A word about control. Kayaks are a little weird. The first few times out you can expect to be paddling along, arms wheeling, good speed, and all of a sudden, for no apparent reason, the kayak will take a sudden twist to the right or left. It apparently has something to do with the hull design and speed attained, but it can be puzzling no matter how normal it might be. A few miles of paddling under your belt and these unexpected twists will bug you less and less, and after a time you get completely used to them.

Backstroke

The backstroke is one way to correct these weird twists. Ordinarily, it's best to get into the habit of using forward strokes as often as possible—anything else slows your momentum. Just pretend at first you don't have a reverse.

On the other hand, a good bold backstroke does have its place, and should be in the paddler's repertoire.

Lower the paddle blade well behind you, power-face *up*—don't change the power-face around for the stroke. The backstroke is done with the blade facing exactly the same as for the forward stroke, which means, if you are using a curved blade, you are using the less efficient side of the paddle. Don't switch around, because the blades should be ready for their primary work, the forward strokes.

Again, the lower blade is behind you. Your upper arm is crossed over your chest, the hand over the side of the boat opposite where it usually is. Keep the elbow of the lower arm directly over the shaft and shove the lower arm down and forward. You'll probably be leaning back when you do this stroke, and again, power the stroke with *both* arms, using leverage.

Paddle-Braces

So far we've covered just the basic strokes—the travelling strokes. That's like telling a track star what it's like to walk. The travelling strokes are what you need to get started.

The real magic of the kayak comes with the lean, and the way a skillfully handled paddle allows the kayaker to break through the craft's instability barrier.

This breakthrough comes with paddle-braces. And the phrase is very descriptive because "bracing" is what it's all about.

Though a bewildering variety of maneuvers fall into the category, paddle-braces in general are for stabilizing the craft. The paddle is usually extended far out from the craft, not so much to move it but to brace, to provide an outrigger effect.

In the execution of the brace, the most common problem for the beginner is the failure to keep the leading edge of the paddle blade angled upwards.

As you raise the leading edge out flat on the water, the water exerts lifts on the paddle and the kayak is pushed back up. You can, indeed, tilt or lean the kayak practically on edge and then depend on that uplift—water against paddle—to stabilize you. The problem is that it takes a lot of concentration, a subtle feel for the paddle, to avoid plunging the leading edge downward and pulling the kayak on over.

Once this subtlety is mastered, you can do all sorts of things with it.

One of the more interesting of the maneuvers allowed by the brace is the "Duffek Turn", a turn named after Milovan Duffek, a Czech who developed it back in the early Fifties. The effect of the turn can be favorably compared to running wide open down the sidewalk and suddenly reaching out and grabbing a light pole.

The Duffek turn is both a brace and turning maneuver. The kayak speeds forward. The blade is extended either right or left, and hits the water with the blade-face angled, leading edge up, about 45 degrees against the water's onrush.

As the blade is planted, firmly, with good downward arm pressure, the kayak will take a quick 90° to 180° spin around the paddle—just as you would do when running and grabbing the light pole. In this case the paddle becomes not only a brace, but a pivot as well.

Such a wide—and initially confusing—variety of strokes and braces is not due entirely to the tendency of people with specialties to develop jargon. It's not all jargon, not at all. Each of the strokes and/or maneuvers is a little different, does a slightly different job. There's the front brace, back brace, low and high braces, sculling brace, just as there are forward and back strokes, sculling strokes, sweep and draw strokes.

And each of these could be described, and some comment made about how various combinations of them work together. The classic example of how they interact, for instance, is that the basic draw stroke is affected drastically by a lean, and varies if you're leaning towards or away from the draw. You'll have to know these combinations if you're going to race or rally kayaks. But going over each of the named strokes or maneuvers at this point would prove little except confusing. It would take several hundred pages and underline only the simple truth: once you're in the kayak, practice, and still more practice, is what's needed. If you're going to get serious about competing, you should find a coach and really work it out. Fancy terminology won't help until then.

Instead we're going to wrap up the paddling section with a discussion of how to use lean and currents, and two refinements of basic maneuvers to show the principles involved. Working refinements into all your kayaking can only come with serious effort and long work—practice.

Sculling Stroke

The purpose for describing the sculling stroke over some others is that it allows nothing less than a rather incredible lean, allowing you to further use the lean to do other maneuvers.

The stroke begins with a strong lean—either forced or voluntary. The paddler extends the paddle and, just under the surface of the water, describes horizontal figure eights with the blade. These are done slowly, but with force. You'll be surprised at how well this single stroke can help you control the boat in current or waves.

Current

When broadside or quartering across a current, a fast current, expose the bottom of the kayak to the pressure of the water. Lean away from the current slightly. If this isn't done, the current grabs the deck and might flip the craft over sideways. Perhaps this sounds as if it's a very simple point, and it is. But it's a point that has to be remembered in an almost infinite variety of situations— often when it's not the most obvious thing to have on your mind. Make certain that you know—again, automatically —how you and the kayak work together in current. Practise this until you don't have to think about it when you're in a tight situation.

Incidentally, it's possible to use the current for "ferrying," which is the name given to slipping sideways across the current. All you do is expose the bottom of the boat to the oncoming current—with the bow slightly down- or upstream. The current will propel you, "slide" you across the stream or river.

Again, and always, remember that there is only one way to truly learn kayaking—practice and more practice. After you get good at the basic maneuvers in calm waters, the turns and braces and strokes and Eskimo roll (*Esquimautage* in jargon), after you think you've got it all down, then do it some more. Don't try anything rough, any whitewater of any kind, until you are absolutely positive that you are good enough. Even then get a qualified coach or judge or experienced kayaker to test you out.

You can't be too good.

Some safety notes, both general and special to kayaking.

Don't kayak without flotation bags, and if dumped and forced to wet-exit, keep the kayak downstream from you.

If you're in a group, go quickly for any kayak which is hullside up and shows no sign of movement or activity. Whoever is underneath can have been knocked unconscious—it happens more often than you'd think. Get there fast, get the person out and give mouth-to-mouth if needed.

If you're aboard and an endangered victim is in the water, give the stern of your boat, not the side—it's easy to tip you from the side. Have the person take hold of the stern grabloop and do side stroke if possible, kicking the legs to bring the body horizontal—a vertical dead weight creates a drag almost impossible to paddle against.

Always rescue people and get them to shore before going for equipment. Always.

If the water is at all cold, or if there are any signs *at all* of shivering, build a fire and get the victim warm.

Don't run rapids or wildwater alone. And even when you take somebody with you, leave word where you'll be, and when you expect to get back. File a "flight plan" for the trip with your parents before you leave.

Never run a stretch without scouting it first, even stretches with which you're basically familiar. A storm may have altered the pattern of the river since you saw it last.

If you reach an area you're not convinced you can handle, portage around it.

As a last thought: in kayaking circles it's considered very bad form to get into serious trouble—a failure to consider your own and anybody else's safety.

CHAPTER 9

Rafts, Rafting

In reality, while rafting is fun and a very definite water-crafting sport, it's difficult to get into it the way you can kayaking and canoeing.

Part of the problem is the expense. A good-sized river-running raft can go close to a stunning fifteen hundred dollars—without oars. And for your average bear that runs into a pile of money just to run a bit of wildwater.

Then, too, there's the complication and limited application of rafting. You can't just throw one on top of the car, as you can a canoe or kayak, and have an afternoon of stooging around on a calm lake or river. Rafts paddle like bricks, and simply aren't handy to use.

So this section will be confined to conservative approaches to rafting trips—where a group of not-rich-people can pool their funds and rent a raft for an exploration of some wildwater. We'll cover the kinds of things to watch for when taking a whitewater cruise with commercial outfitters. And we'll talk of rivers.

As an indication of what is happening to river rafting, it

117

might help to look at the mighty Colorado. Until 1949 about a hundred people, *total*, had plunged through its awesome rapids. Now traffic is so heavy, especially through the Grand Canyon stretch, that private permits are almost impossible to come by—now the permit structure is so rigidly controlled that it approaches being a flat refusal. You must have three 10-man rafts to a party, at least one experienced boatman on each raft, one person in the party who has previously shot the Colorado, and then file your application at least six months ahead of time.

The Colorado is a rough river. It begins in Wyoming and Colorado and crashes through canyons in Utah and through 218 miles of the Grand Canyon in Arizona—a wild, rock-ripped, thundering river.

The direct reason for the sudden rise in the popularity of the Colorado is that someone discovered the rubber raft, previously limited to ocean survival work. These rafts have a feature no other river craft has: they are very flexible. They can cling to the water even when it's very wild. If the water shoots up, so does the raft, bending to take the shock. If it drops, the raft follows. If the river throws the raft into a boulder, the raft gives—it rolls with the punishment and takes blows which would shatter a more rigid craft. As a matter of fact, the raft is probably the safest and easiest of the wildwater boats. That doesn't mean mistakes are impossible. Now and then they'll flip (called "pancaking") and dump everybody. Sometimes they will get punctured, though most of them have several different air tanks so they don't sink. But compared to canoes and kayaks, the raft is an apartment on the water— albeit sometimes a lively one.

It is also a wonderful way to romp down a river.

DO-IT-YOURSELF RAFTERS

For those who are going to do limited rafting on their own, at limited expense, there are some things to know and other things to avoid if maximum enjoyment is to be had.

First, match the raft to the water and your ability. If you're just going to gig around in a pool or small pond, then one of those cheap discount-store, two-man rafts will do it. Don't expect the raft to last more than one season, however, and don't try anything more than that pool or pond with it.

For any other use, any river or lake or even mildly rough water, go with a tougher raft, and learn more about rafting.

Initially, the most confusing feature about buying a decent rubber raft is understanding the capacity rating of rubber rafts. The rafts we use on the rivers for sport are closely related to the survival rafts and the old survival ratings are still used. The 5-man raft *will* float five people —on the ocean, crowded together awaiting rescue. Down a river with a few curls, a five-man raft will only take two people and a minimal amount of camping gear. It takes at least a six-man raft to haul two people with a lot of gear for a long trip. So buy accordingly. Don't try to make less do for more—it'll only disappoint you and let you down in the pinch.

It's the same on weight ratings—those figures are maximums. For river work, even mild rivers, cut the ratings by at least a third—and a half wouldn't be out of line. And don't forget to count the weight of everything which will be in the raft when checking against the ratings: gear, food, the rowing frame if there is one, the oars, the weight of passengers. It all counts.

Then assess the quality. Again, for playing around, the little discount-store raft is fun. But for rivers, you've got to get serious; for anything more than just playing around steer clear of the thin-skinned, lightweight neoprene-coated nylons and cottons. Sometimes a mere bump against a sharp rock will pop a raft of this material.

Costing a bit more, but much tougher, is polyvinyl chloride (P.V.C.). Get a raft of P.V.C. that is double-layered and laminated—which is common—and you've got a pretty tough raft. You'll find P.V.C. making up all the smallish rectangular rafts and also the inflatable kayaks. While they are fairly sturdy, they, too, should be kept away from long stretches full of sharp rocks.

The truly large rafts—the ones which cost up to fifteen hundred dollars—go back to the neoprene-coated nylons but are much more heavily constructed than the small cheap rafts.

So, if you're buying for a long, rough trip, go with the big rafts with the heavy neoprene-coated nylon (cotton will rot out over long periods), and for the smaller trips, the P.V.C.

It perhaps should be added here that after research the authors can't recommend that you get your own raft and start taking trips. It is, on rough whitewater, a definite life-endangering situation if you aren't properly trained and/or with a competent rafter.

We understand, however, that many who read will want to get their own and for those who persist, we publish the following guidelines:

Buying a used raft is, at best, a tricky affair. It's possible to get a good deal, but extreme care must be taken when buying. Unless you know the dealer, or are buying it from a friend, be absolutely cautious before purchasing.

Check along the seams first, for bad cuts and/or abrasions. Sometimes rough wear—pulling on gravel, folding the raft with small rocks buried in the seams—will do damage.

Inflate the raft before you buy, of course, and check it. If you can, douse it with a soap and water solution. Each bubble that appears will be a leak. The bubbles don't catch all the leaks—there will perhaps be some which won't be discovered until later. Leaks can be repaired, of course, but if you're looking at a whole raft full of leaks you should reconsider. It might be that the raft has been poorly used and not worth buying.

Don't buy a raft with tubes smaller than 16 or 17 inches in diameter. Anything smaller is inadequate for any kind of whitewater. Also, stick to at least 24-ounce neoprene-nylon, with something heavier for the raft floor. While the floors aren't a big safety consideration, it's best to have the heavier construction.

Don't buy a raft unless it has at least two flotation chambers. More is still better. Anything less is a sign of particularly thoughtless construction—makes the raft great for serious work in a bathtub, and that's about it.

As to weight of material: the seven-man, similar to six-man but about a foot wider, should be about eighty pounds, maybe a little heavier. Anything less is too cheap.

Following these guidelines is, really, just common sense. The most important thing to remember about getting into rafting by buying your own raft, is that just getting the raft is a bare start. Owning the raft doesn't qualify you for a whitewater run, not until you've studied the waters a lot more, and taken time to talk—one on one—with whitewater pilots who *know* what they're doing. Don't, whatever you do, just get the raft and hit the wildwater. That's the surest way to disaster that you can find. Doing your own rafting is difficult in that you must take an excessive amount of time to learn how to use them, how to work them down a river, studying with other people, before you get a chance to try them out for yourself. We will, of course, cover paddling and reading some of the whitewater you'll encounter but it will only be a kind of introduction. If you're going to get into rafting you'll have to study more and with many experts, to really *know* what you're doing, otherwise there is much danger.

MOVING THE RAFT

There is a thought, common in amateurs, that you simply put the raft in the water, nudge it out into the current and hang on until it squirts out the bottom of the canyon: the old wild ride on the wild river concept.

The truth is that the raft must be steered, and rowed, or it will flop and go under before the first turn. Large sweep oars and motors move the big commercial rafts for guided trips or for ocean-going work, and we'll skip them here. Oars and paddles move the private owners' rafts.

Paddling is the most difficult, the most time-consuming and the least productive. On the other hand, it is the cheapest, and you needn't build or buy a rowing frame (more of which later).

The paddling technique of rafting is basically anything that will get the big pile of rubber moving. And they move very slowly. In still, calm water—a pond, with no wind—a rafter can't expect to exceed two miles an hour, and that only for a short time before fatigue sets in.

If you hit still water and have to paddle any length of

time, the best method is to straddle the tube, one on each side, or more if there's room, and just keep paddling. You'll note that the rubber seems to absorb most of the energy you're applying and that the raft seems to drag a lot on the water. Both of these indications are absolutely true—rafts absorb energy and drag a lot. And if you must go any distance using paddles for power you'll find that it absolutely wrecks you to paddle them; it is an exhausting experience.

A trick that helps: sit up on the tube backwards to the direction you wish to go. Pin the shaft of the paddle against your hip with your hand functioning as an oarlock and "row" with the paddle. It's really much faster and easier and saves tired muscles.

For large rafts with several people on them, team paddling is a necessity. Somebody who knows the river is selected as a "captain" and he or she sits in the rear and watches ahead. The commands are very simple and basic. *Ahead, behind,* and *left* and *right* for turns. On *left,* everybody on the left side paddles, on *right* the opposite. (Note: on team paddling, be sure to balance the boat as far as weight and strength are concerned. If all the brutes are on one side, you'll spend the whole trip leaning while you go in circles.)

Two other strokes for the team paddlers: the team *draw,* and the team *pry.* This is to move the raft sideways as straight and fast as possible. On the command of *draw right,* all those on the right side will do a draw or reaching stroke to the right while those on the left perform a prying stroke—jamming the paddle down vertically, and pulling over on the top to kick the flat blade out at the bottom. This maneuver slides the whole raft sideways across the water and is very good for fast lateral moves to miss large rocks in the middle of the current.

It is also, in a limited way, possible to "ferry" the raft, much as with the kayak, using the current. This is an easy way to get around obstacles which are still some distance away. All you do is lean *towards* the current, and paddle at a 45 degree angle upstream—in a tangent across the water. The current will act against the direction of paddling to produce the ferrying effect. The maneuver can be done either upstream or down, so long as you lean across the water at an angle.

Other methods of moving the raft, personal quirks of your own raft, will become evident as you work in water. But a final note of caution about paddling, or any use of a raft for that matter: getting wet is part of the game. In chilly weather getting wet can be downright dangerous, bringing your temperature down. Consider water temperature before setting out, and be prepared to stop and build a fire to warm any chilled crew members.

ROWING; USING OARS

Before getting into a discussion of rowing, it is necessary to re-examine your equipment with hard use in mind. Many rafts come with oarlocks more or less imbedded in the material, cute little metal rings and the like. They are, at the very best, mostly for show. To work a river seriously with a raft and oars, it's necessary to buy or build a rowing frame. This is a wooden frame which runs around the top of the raft, lashed into place, with oarlocks in drilled holes in blocks of wood put in for that purpose. (See the illustration.)

Do not try any serious rowing on any kind of water without a good rowing frame. Rubber sides without a frame have a tendency to collapse, to give with each stroke, so you lose power. Also, working the oars against the rubber wears away the material.

With the frame lashed in place, it is time to take another look at the whole concept of rowing.

Conventional rowing puts your back to the direction you're going, with the bow also in back of you. That's fine on lakes, perhaps, or in ocean dory situations, but not so good where a huge boulder might be waiting just around the next bend.

In the very late 1800s a man named Nathan Galloway discovered that the best way to row down rough rivers included facing downstream, so you can see where you're going. Galloway swung his stern around so it was facing downstream, and then rowed *upstream*, against the current. This doubles steering ability, and gives you an extra moment or two to react because it slows your down-current race slightly.

Until you get used to them oars will feel very awkward— sort of trying to lift a rock with a lever which is pulling sideways all the time.

Get the hang of it all on still water. Rowing in any kind of moving water throws the additional push-pull of current into the equation, which complicates things immensely. So master the basics before moving to the heavier stuff . . .

In the beginning, always try to keep the blade or face of the oar perpendicular to the water. Slice down into the water as if you were slicing a cake. Later you may want to learn to feather them—turn the blades sideways—to miss an underwater obstacle, but at first hold them straight up and down.

Then practise rowing a straight course. It's not unusual for beginning oarsmen to find that one side of their body

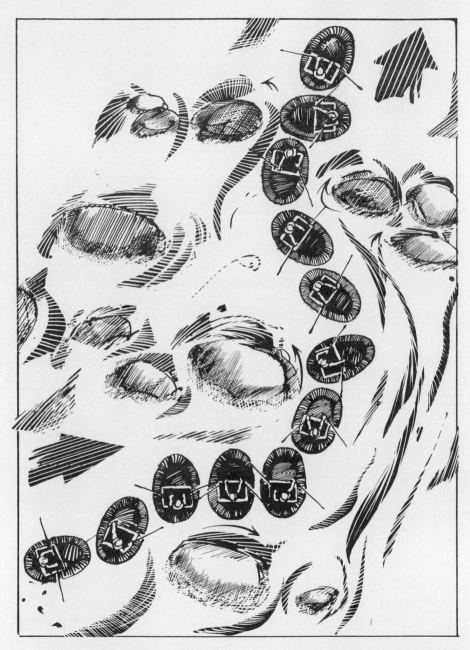

Oar Techniques Through Rapids

is stronger than the other, pulling the raft to that side, and sometimes it takes a while to guide the raft in a direct line.

Once you're competent at the straight ahead rowing, practise a little back-rowing—just to know how and to loosen those new muscles which are popping. Then, with forwards and backwards rowing down pat, it's time for the most maddening maneuver of all: the double-oar turn.

If you pull on one oar only, the boat will turn. But if you pull on one oar while pushing on the other, it will turn twice as fast: the double-oar turn.

All you do is push on one oar while pulling on the other. It's that basic. But it can drive you crazy until you work it out. For some reason the body always expects the boat to turn the opposite way from which it does turn.

But, along with normal rowing the double-oar turn is an absolute necessity. Work on it, deal with it until you can close your eyes and pin that bow down on a dime in an instant and you just might be ready for a little white—or at least frothy—water.

Later there's a chapter on whitewater, but for now it's only necessary to know that in almost all situations, the basic raft maneuver is the ferry.

Know the upstream ferry, and the down. Find some slow current at first and work hard to master both ferrying methods, going across at a 45 degree angle. It is the one maneuver which will keep you out of trouble, the one which you should work at the most.

If you are going downstream, in the middle, and the ferry didn't work, nor the draw, and you are obviously going to crash into a boulder, move *towards* the rock. The natural tendency is to move away from an impending collision, but it's wrong. If you move away you will bring the up-current side of the raft down, and the current can get

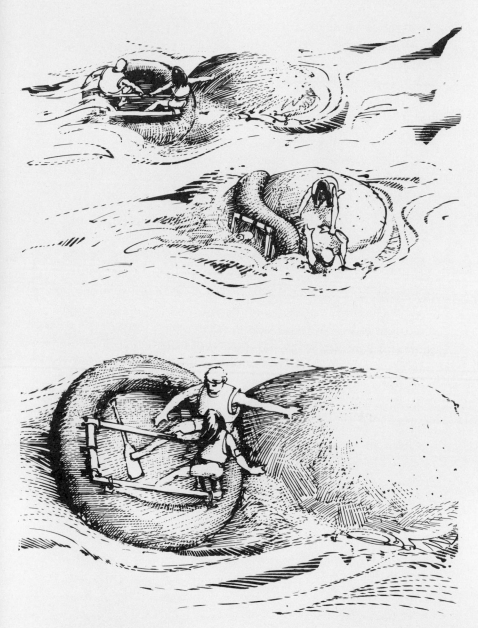

Raft Approaching Rock

hold of it and take it under. Keep that edge up, so the current will go under it, and you can use your arms to work the raft around the rock or boulder.

Life vests are, of course, an absolute must. But don't rely on the life vest to save you from everything—use your head. If you should get thrown out of the raft, get away from it to avoid getting hit by an oar. If you are pushed and held under the water, get to the surface as fast as possible, pulling evenly and with steady force to get up out of any down-pull.

Then position yourself so your legs are downstream. You don't want your head or trunk to take collisions with rocks. Take them with your feet. Have your legs out in front, raised, and with your knees slightly bent to absorb shock.

Work to shore and a calm place as soon as you can, then wait for help. *Don't* try to swim on down and through any really bad rapids—it is extremely dangerous.

Some other general raft safety notes:

All the usual safety rules apply, the same as to all boating. So check to make certain everybody in your party can swim, can hold their breath for an extended period of time (a minute), and knows how to administer water first aid.

Try to keep water bailed out of the raft. It can accumulate and add great weight to the cargo load.

Never, under any circumstances, raft in high water, flood water, or spring runoff. Not only is runoff or flood water hard and fast, it usually carries trash, debris, logs, which can gut a raft and cause you bodily injury. Wait until the water is settled. Talk to the rangers and river people, get all the information you can about the water and water level before you go.

Don't raft in the dark. While that would appear stunningly obvious, it is amazing the number of people who actually try to raft when the sun is gone.

And finally, remember that when/if an accident occurs, people always come first. Don't think about equipment until everybody is safe.

GUIDED TRIPS

There is really very little to say about guided rafting trips except the obvious: be certain the trip you are on is being run by competent pros who know the river you're doing.

Perhaps it is sad, but cousin Elbert who once shot half a mile of mild water on the Green out in Utah just isn't qualified to take you on a ten day run down the Colorado. Period. And if you try it you're going to have a life-endangering situation on your hands before you get around the first bend.

Be sure that you are talking to experts; don't be embarrassed to check around a little to make sure they're valid. If they are they will furnish references without a hassle.

And then, once you have decided to go with them, don't hassle them. Do as they say, lean back and enjoy the trip.

CHAPTER 10

Whitewater: Understanding It

Whitewater, thundering, roaring—a wildness that takes your breath away, utterly powerful . . .

With the possible exception of the sea, which is truly mighty, in no other area of water use is there such a need for knowledge as there is in using whitewater—whether you're kayaking, canoeing or rafting.

Fortunately, there are ways to understand whitewater, ways to use it, and experts who can supply all the help you'll need for at least a start, a knowledge base to build upon.

And it starts with something called the International Scale—which is a scale to rate the difficulty of rapids and rivers either here or in Europe. While it is primarily for kayakers, the scale works for rafters as well. It is a scale from I to VI, I being easy, VI being impossible.

For more localized help, you may want to use the 1 to 10 scale of Leslie Allen Jones, Star Route Box 13A, Heber City, Utah, 84032. Jones makes river maps the likes of which you can't find anywhere else. Anyone who is considering any kind of river travel through heavy water would do well to get in touch with Jones.

Jones' scale is known also as the Western Scale, and it

might be wise to take a moment to compare it to the International Scale. There is some difference of opinion coming in around classes V and VI of the International Scale. Some Europeans, for example, reserve the Class VI designation for rapids which have yet to be successfully run. Others equate Class VI with Jones' 10, which is reserved for rapids that will capsize one of every two boats trying to run them—when those two boats are the best craft being handled by experts.

You must form your own opinions, of course. And to help, we are publishing both scales below. You can argue later when you are a pro.

International Scale	Western Rapid Rating
I =	0—Flatwater. Lakes. Storms don't count here.
	1-2—Easy. Slight gradient. Current slow to moderate. The channel is wide and easy to follow. Few obstructions. Waves up to a foot high and generally easy to avoid. Okay for beginners.
II =	3-4—Moderate. Faster current. You can still find the channel. Some obstructions. Waves up to a couple of feet. Does require decent equipment and basic whitewater experience and skills.
III =	5-6—Difficult. Heavy current. Takes skill to find the channel. Waves up to three feet. Scouting usually necessary, definitely for the first run. Skilled operator with good equipment necessary. The absolute top limit for open canoes, no matter how good you are.
IV =	7-8—Bad stuff. Rescue difficult. Long, vio-

lent rapids. Obstructed channels with passages turbulent and requiring expert maneuvering.

V   =   9-10—Life-risking river—*only* for teams of experts testing well-honed skills. Huge drops, violent suckholes, extremely steep gradients.

VI =   U—Unrunnable. Period.

Usually, those who are starting stay down with the lower numbers and practise until they get good enough to work up. The exception to this is when you rent an outfitter and take a rafting trip down a river with pros.

The true value in the chart, or any other measurement of whitewater, is in measuring it against your own abilities. Know yourself. And no matter what a chart might say, if you look at a stretch of river and it looks to be too much for your skill—stay away from it.

Then, too, the ratings listed in various books and charts and maps are based on certain stages of the rivers. Hit the same river at a time when it's not usually run and all sorts of things will be different—including the rating. Certain very measurable things go into the rating: gradient, which is how much the river drops over a given distance; and volume, which tells how much water flows past a given point in a given time. On a huge river, the volume can be immense and the paddling very quiet and easy. But down a tight rock chute a relatively small variation in the volume may make all the difference in the world. Gradient can be constant, in which case the rapids will deserve a single rating throughout, or it can be highly irregular, and you'll find stretches of placid water interspersed with stretches of mad and potentially dangerous wildwater.

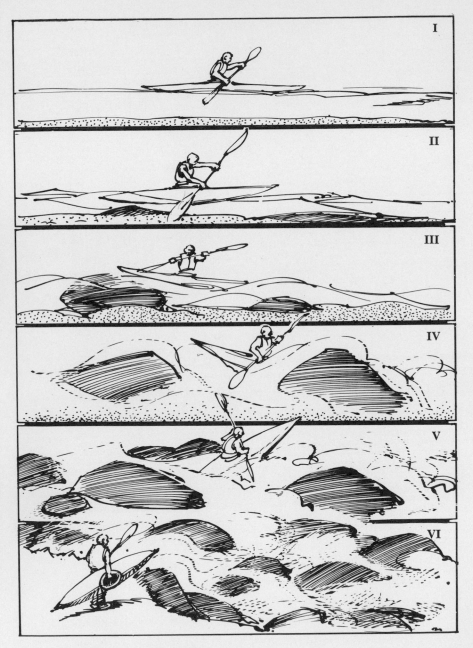

International Rapid Scale

Also, if the ratings do tend to be based on the worst stretches of the river in question, they still don't always tell you what you need to know. In reality, the ratings generally indicate the degree of maneuvering skill required to tackle a given stretch. But if the river is cresting, many of the rapids might be under three feet of fast moving but smooth water. All you have to do is get through without having the bottom of your kayak ripped out by floating debris.

For any kind of whitewater work, whether there are ratings or not, there is simply no substitute for first hand knowledge and experience. And if you ever intend playing in any water rougher than a II, a thorough working knowledge of the way water functions in rapids is absolutely mandatory.

Fortunately, when all factors are known and accounted for, the action of running water—even in a wild river—is entirely predictable. Running water, like all water, obeys the laws of physics. Given money and time, you could actually make a small stretch of whitewater in a laboratory and it would perform exactly as the big river.

The only problem is that in the laboratory conditions are never quite the same as on the riverbed. The variety of play, the variations of current on a riverbed are for all practical purposes infinite. And the main attitude when studying whitewater should be caution: never underestimate the power and complexity that changing factors can introduce. Don't read a few pages about the way water works and think you can jump right into some Class 3 water.

Following are the basics. They'll get you started, but no more. They are only meant as a springboard for more detailed study later on. They'll get you to Level II. We urge you to study, to talk to professional river people before going above Level II.

First, imagine an inclined trough, raised at one end. Now imagine water being poured down through the trough. Several things will happen to the water.

Because of friction with the trough, the water will be slowest at the bottom. The trough will actually try to hold it back a little. The same goes, in a more limited way, for the top because of friction with the air. But in the middle, high in the middle, the water will move fastest because against other water, moving water has very little friction.

There will also, obviously, be some friction of the water against the sides of the trough, and this creates a strange-looking phenomenon. There will be a corkscrew current running down the sides of the trough, a spinning tube of current on each side of the main stream. On the surface these corkscrew currents tend to throw debris into the middle of the stream. But on the bottom they're spinning in the opposite direction—spinning up the bank to the outside as they twirl downstream. This twirling motion is called *helical flow*. Generally, in fast running water, you can expect to almost always find a main current near the middle and the slower moving helical flow on both sides. The most obvious effect is that surface debris—including kayaks and paddles—tends to get shoved out into the middle of the stream while anything that sinks gets sucked over to the side.

Also, conditions may vary enough so that helical flow is diminished beyond recognition. In shallow water, for instance, there may either not be enough room for the helical flow to be very pronounced, or the riverbed may be irregular enough and close enough to the surface so that other effects are more powerful and prominent.

Our imaginary trough implies a straight-line flow. A river, on the other hand, goes around bends and curves. Since water is heavy and the main channel flow has a pressure of its own, the helical flow on the outside of the curve gets "squashed". On a sharp curve with the water moving fast, the helical current literally gets nailed to the outside wall. And on the inside of the curve the helical current will expand. Sometimes it will expand clear over to the other side.

Then, after the river rounds the bend, all the currents which have mixed have to fight and swirl around until they have room to get themselves sorted out again.

All right—so far we've assumed that the flow in the trough is regular and constant, that the gradient or down-slope is steady, that there are no curves and no obstructions to the flow and that the width of the trough holds steady.

Of course, in a river all these factors are constantly shifting. As gradient increases, the speed of the water will do likewise. Or when the channel narrows, it will squeeze the currents, increase pressures. Or, twists and turns will modify other currents, change them to meet particular demands. Obstacles—boulders—will change everything once again.

A boulder under water, with room over the top for you to pass, can still prove bothersome. As the water comes down on the boulder it is forced up and over the top, making a bulge of water on the surface. This bulge is called a "surge." And it's a good thing to recognize surges and pull your paddle up as you go over to keep from hitting the boulder and damaging your paddle.

Some surges are called "sleepers," and that's when the boulder is so close to the surface that it will take the hull of your boat—yet it will appear minimal. For this reason it's best to go around all surges.

Now, just downstream of the boulder, just over the top as the current comes, there will be a depression beyond the boulder. Water from the sides and top flows into this depression, trying to fill this hole; it even kicks back from downstream.

This coming-back of the water causes a downward current, viciously cutting down the face of the boulder, then out at the bottom and back up to the surface and back in and down the rock face again: a head-over-heels, circling current.

If the rock is small the depression and down-current won't do much more than slow you down a bit. But if the current is fast, the river big and the boulder huge—as is the case in most whitewater—there is great danger. The depression is then called a "suckhole." If a person in a life jacket is caught in one of these suckholes, it's possible to be trapped. The current pulls you down, but the flotation of the vest won't let you go all the way down to the bottom of the current-swirl and around back up the surface. You hang there until you can fight your way out to the side and back into the current. It's an experience which can make you appreciate air a great deal.

Sometimes above these suckholes there will be large standing waves called "haystacks." Haystacks can give you a warning of an oncoming bad suckhole. But at other times there's nothing but a huge, ominous "lift" in the surface of the water to indicate that something dangerous awaits.

Similar swirls happen anywhere that water is dumped in great quantities. If, for instance, the channel suddenly narrows and widens rapidly, swirls will appear where the water is "let out" of the chute.

You will also find swirls at the bottom of a waterfall and that brings up a note of caution: waterfalls are definitely *out*! Do not, under any circumstances, *ever* try to shoot a dam or waterfalls. It is nothing short of suicidal.

If you happen to be on a stretch of water which—for some reason—you haven't been able to scout, watch where water becomes almost deceptively quiet or placid. The water seems to get the quietest above a big drop or falls, gathering the tremendous energies it will expend at the bottom. If you see such a quiet place, or even *think* there might be a falls, get to shore at once. Immediately. And portage around.

Watch for a faint straight line, almost a false horizon, with calm water above and rough water out the other side. Get to shore at once, and portage around the falls or drop (also called a "weir").

But not all the things you look for ahead on the river are bad. One of the nice things to find is a "V" shape in the water. All the water around it is frothy, torn up a bit, but that V just lies there—rather still in comparison to the water around it. You enter the V at the top, at the opening, and funnel on down into its narrowest part. The V acts like any arrow, pointing the way you want to go, and it shows in a variety of situations.

Remember, for instance, how heavy or fast current rounds a bend? The helical flow on the outside is crushed under the weight of the current and on the inside the other helical twist grows? So the V points right to where the fastest current is—to the outside. If you let that V be your guide you'll outrun anybody trying to cut corners; your competition will be caught up in the helical flow and you'll squirt on through.

Fastwater eddies are something else you must watch out for—and can use.

When a boulder sticks up out of the water, and the water is forced to rush around to the sides, eddies are formed just downstream, kind of tucked into the boulder.

Unlike suckholes, if the eddies aren't obviously totally wild, they aren't dangerous. As a matter of fact they're very handy to use because in an eddy there is no downward current pull. It is possible to slide into a boulder eddy, or an eddy formed by a side wall or sandbar, and relax and rest long enough to look over forthcoming rapids.

Eddies are also like playgrounds in that one of the primary enjoyments of kayaking is trying to downriver jump from eddy to eddy, squirting into the V's and riding the jets of water downstream.

A few words in passing about whitewater in general. It is an almost indescribable joy, at times, to ride something as wild as a thundering river. It has been called the ultimate outdoor experience, an adrenalin high, a soul-shaking down-rip that leaves your breath permanently about two miles in back of you.

More, riding the wildwater can and often does give you a new look at yourself. It shows you how to overcome fear, makes you a more whole person—a tested person who has won.

Whitewater can do all that.

But whitewater is also exceedingly dangerous, particularly if attempted without proper knowledge and study. It can be dangerous even for experts—experts make mistakes. And if you are not an expert, it's quite possible to endanger your life through sheer ignorance, pushing danger to the critical level without even knowing you are doing so.

Safety—both in knowledge and equipment—is absolutely necessary. Always. Life vests, helmets, knowledge, the ability to swim well and hold your breath for nearly a minute—all of these things are vital. Reading the water, thorough practice with your body and boat, an intimate knowledge of how rapids function—it is *all* necessary, all imperative if you are to be safe. And it is all, all of it together, only a start.

Learn more, learn as much as you can, before you slide that bow into a downriver chute and start. Then you can appreciate more, enjoy more, without the weight of concern hanging over you.

CHAPTER 11

Repairs

There are, for any given damage, three kinds of repair: emergency, temporary (or field), and permanent (at home).

Of course they vary tremendously with the kind of material, kind of boat, kind of water and kind of situation. It could, in fact, be said that no two repairs are the same—and for that reason it's a little tricky to pin down repair methods. But there are some things which hold true long enough to at least nail down a procedure or two.

Methods are listed below. But remember that nothing is iron hard—flex these things to fit your own situation.

EMERGENCY REPAIRS

In any emergency situation, the primary drive is the same: stabilize through control.

The only damage which can cause an emergency, obviously, is damage which causes a hole in the hull or structural breakage of one kind or another. Usually a rock, snag or log will puncture or rip the hull.

Jam anything you can find in the hole. Cushions, jackets, spare life vest, anything that will impede the flow of in-

145

coming water. Just react. Jam something in the hole. Then, if there are two of you, one should start bailing while the other heads for shore.

Do not waste time talking, thinking, or speculating. Get a plug in the hole, start bailing, and head for shore. Water will rush into a hole at a truly alarming rate—sinking you in seconds.

In a kayak, get out. Don't try to ride it out. Get out, jam something into the hole if you can and pull the boat to shore.

If it's a rubber raft and one of the air containers is punctured, stay with it—it'll still float—and paddle or row to shore.

The main thing is to react quickly. Seconds count. Stabilize the damage, stop or impede the inward flow of water, and get to some kind of solid ground.

FIELD REPAIR

Once emergency repair has been done and you are on shore there is time to do a field repair. Here the basic thought is not looks, but usability.

Always carry a can of fiberglass putty, with a small tube of catalyst, and a small (about a foot square) piece of fiberglass cloth. Tuck them under a seat. A pint can of putty will do it, and you don't need any tools—a stick will do. This stuff is too thick and brittle for permanent repairs, too hard to make the result look nice and polished, but for temporary repairs it can't be beat.

On land, turn the damaged spot up and let it dry out for an hour or so in the sun. You want *all* water out, of both sides of the damage.

When it's all dry, mix some of the fiberglass putty—just about two tablespoons—with a little of the catalyst. Full instructions come on the can, but it helps to make it just a *tiny* bit "hot"—a half a drop extra catalyst.

Using this small amount of the putty, glue the damaged pieces of hull (whether it be glass, aluminum, wood or canvas, but not rubber) back together. It will be impossible to do perfectly, but try to make all the pieces stick back together. Work fast. Once the catalyst triggers the stuff, it's just a few minutes to hardening.

Now, with the hull pieces pulled back into position and glued—messy and ragged—let it dry for ten or fifteen minutes so it sets up well after it hardens.

Next take out the fiberglass cloth. Then mix up another batch of the putty, this time enough to cover the whole damaged area $\frac{1}{16}''$ deep. Immediately, before it hardens, spread the cloth out over the putty, pressing it down and working it smoothly into the still-wet goop. Make certain it sticks all around, and across the middle, rubbing it in with the flat part of a stick.

Again, let the fiberglass putty dry well—good and hard, totally set.

And, finally, mix up the rest of the putty and cover the whole patch area, cloth and all, with another layer to bond or laminate the patch in. Smooth with the stick as best you can.

It isn't pretty. And as a matter of fact it's not as strong as it could be—or will be when you can get home and do a permanent repair. But it will serve, let you finish the trip and take a surprising amount of punishment before coming apart.

If for some reason you didn't bring putty, a hasty patch

can be accomplished with a poncho or waterproof blanket. Double the poncho once, then wrap it all around the whole canoe or kayak and tie it at the top—not unlike a giant bandage—with the poncho pulled tight across the damaged area. It has to be very tight, and it will still leak a little, but it will keep the main flow of water out until you can get home—though it makes paddling a bear.

PERMANENT (HOME) REPAIR

The key word with any decent boat repair, at least if it's going to look nice and be structurally sound, is patience. Unlike the emergency or field repair, at home there is time to take care—so think slow.

First, if it had been an emergency or field repair, tear out the temporarily fixed portion and get back down to the damaged area.

Then evaluate the extent of the damage. If it is simply a small hole then a laminate patch will do it. But be sure there isn't any lateral or cross-boat structural strain or damage. (This can be readily seen by studying the fiberglass for a crushed or strained appearance.)

Specific methods are listed below.

Wood and/or Wood-Canvas Canoes

First check the stringers, the wooden strips which hold the skin. If any are broken they must be repaired, obviously. Do this by carefully cutting out the broken section of wood, then cut a new piece to fit the hole. Of course it won't just hang there, so back it up with another piece of stringer, a foot longer, and glue this new piece over the whole old section with a good waterproof glue. The new, laminated stringer piece will be stronger than the old.

As for the skin, whether it be canvas or glass, the repair is the same. Go to the fiberglass section for instructions.

If the skin is wood—or you have a wooden hulled canoe —you must rip out the whole old stringer. Clean the gap well, insert a new stringer, and use both wood screws and glue to hold it in place.

Fiberglass (synthetics) Repair

A cautionary note: if you have one of those super-thin-skinned lightweight racing machines, it's probably best not to do your own permanent repair unless you are a real pro at working with glass. It's possible to mess up a good hull when it's very thin. You can ruin the smoothness which in turn will cause turbulence and actually slow you down.

For regular synthetic hulls, after any field patch is torn away, determine the extent of the damage so your patch will cover the whole area. Work the ragged edges of the area to be patched back together.

Then, using a tightly-woven cloth and resin (instructions on the can), laminate a piece of cloth over the entire *inside* area of the damaged place. Make sure that this layer of cloth is sloppy wet and sticks well. (Wear rubber gloves and goggles while working with glass and resin.)

When this sets, go back to the outside of the boat. Sand the whole area to be patched until it is smooth and even. (While doing this step, wear not only rubber gloves and goggles but one of those little paper medical masks or nose and mouth cones as well.)

Now take another thin, tightly woven piece of fiberglass cloth, sloppy wet with resin, and smooth it in place over the outside of the hull in the damaged place. Smooth it out with your hands (gloved) so there are no wrinkles, and let it set. In fact, let it cook at least overnight, and maybe another day if it's been cool. That's the best way to insure that it's hard.

The hull will now be strong, probably stronger than the original. But ugly as a mud fence.

Start sanding. Use a medium-grade sandpaper at first, wrapped around a dry sponge for a sanding block. Use long, even strokes. When it's smooth, change to a fine grade of paper, with a rolled piece of dried towel for a block, and work it some more. It must be incredibly smooth, even at this stage.

When it is *smooth*, wipe with a slightly damp rag to get any dust off and let it dry thoroughly.

Now paint it with another thin coat of resin, let dry and sand. And sand. And sand.

When this coat is dry run your hands down the patch. If there are any rough spots, or any of the cloth-fiber shows above the resin, do another coat. Then sand. And another coat, and sand—until it is impossible to tell where the patch ends and the original hull begins.

Now do the same for the inside of the boat—sanding and coating until it's done. This all sounds very hard, and in a way it is—boring, at any rate—but it's not too demanding. If you have even a modicum of hand-eye coordination and a little skill you can do a very passable job. It might not be quite as good as the pros, but it will be strong, and durable.

Paint to match the rest of the hull with pigmented resin or paint, as you wish. Paint is easier to handle and better for matching color. Pigmented resin is a little tricky to use in that what you see most often isn't what you get. A color that looks right when you mix it will change when it sets. If you use resin, spend some time experimenting on a piece of scrap to get the color at least close.

Rubber Rafts

As might be assumed, there is very little to repairing a rubber raft at home. They come with repair kits, and complete instructions for patching, and it's really very simple to get the job done.

A couple of thoughts which apply particularly to rafts. First, don't try to do too much with the simple patch. If the hole is a tear, or bigger than it seems the patch can handle, take the raft into a professional repair setup and get a hot patch vulcanized into place. Second, the best program of "repair" for a rubber raft is prevention: proper maintenance when storing or travelling on land. Don't fold a raft with rocks or gravel or even sand in the seams or corners, because it will wear through the rubber at the seams. Always deflate thoroughly, fold neatly and store safely.

Aluminum Canoes

Unless you are just one crackerjack metal worker, there is almost no way to repair an aluminum canoe and have it look like anything but a repair job.

Get a piece of aluminum big enough to cover the damaged spot and preshape it with your hands to match the shape of the hull. Before putting the patch in place make sure all the old bent-in, torn or dented pieces of aluminum are pushed back out to resemble their original shape.

Now put a thick layer of caulking material all over the area the patch will cover. Make this a quarter of an inch thick, really gooped on, and when you put the patch on make sure it sits well into the caulking material. Then drill four small holes at the four corners and insert erector-set-size screws to bolt the aluminum patch *tightly* to the hull.

Put screws about every two inches all around, after the four corners are held in place, and file them off round on the inside to keep from snagging. It will look strange, but it will keep water out and won't impede the movement of your hull too much.

There are rivets which can be used in place of screws, and some people try to use them for home repair. But it was found in research that they were very hard to use effectively and some leaking always resulted. It was felt they weren't worth the effort.

Final note: use lock washers on the screws. The caulking, or glue, bonds and holds the patch in place, but sometimes the screws will vibrate or work loose over an extended period of time or with rough usage.

CHAPTER 12

Emergency First Aid

DROWNING AID

Mouth to mouth resuscitation

1. Get the victim stretched out, face up.
2. Clear the mouth. Make sure the tongue hasn't gone back into the throat, blocking air passage. Keep the tongue in place by placing your palm over the victim's chin and holding the tongue down with your thumb.
3. With your other hand, lift the neck and tilt the head back.
4. Now pinch the nose so air won't leak.
5. Seal your mouth around the victim's and blow air into the lungs. Turn your ear to victim's mouth to make sure the air is being released. Repeat this process about twelve times a minute—twenty times a minute for a small child.

Don't quit, even if it takes hours for help to come—and it might.

If you can't get the mouth clear, or don't hear the victim releasing air, seal the mouth with your hand and blow through the victim's nose.

153

Often the victim will throw up. Be mentally ready for this and don't let it make you stop. Keep a rag, a piece of clothing, ready to mop up quickly—clear the mouth, and watch your eyes: the acid in vomitus burns. Work through your squeamishness—it could easily be a question of life or death.

Mouth to Mouth Resuscitation

HYPOTHERMIA

One injury, or problem, that seems to be directly related to watercrafting is that age-old crippler known as over-exposure—called by the new name of hypothermia. It amounts to your body chilling to the point where it can no longer hold its normal temperature.

The main symptom is violent, uncontrollable shivering. Don't ever let the victim get beyond this shivering—he or she can lose touch with reality and it can even prove fatal.

Get the victim warm: in a sleeping bag, build a fire, or pour hot drinks down the throat, or all these things, but get the person *warm*. Get into the sleeping bag also, if necessary, just get the body temperature back up. It might take six or eight hours before the temperature regulation system gets back to normal so don't give up.

Other first aid techniques hold the same as in any other outdoor activity. Make certain you know basic first aid techniques and how to deal with injury, bleeding, shock and heat exhaustion. Look them up, now, before you need them.

Hypothermia Treatment

Bibliography

Canoeing. American Red Cross.

Canoe Camping. E. W. Handel; The Ronald Press Co., New York.

Canoeing Manual. New England Camping Association, Boston.

Cockleshell Heroes. C. E. Lucas Phillips; Heinemann. (Read this for fun, to see what has been done in a kayak during war.)

Elements of Canoeing. P. V. Pulling; Ann Arbor Press, Michigan.

Living Canoeing. A. W. Byde; A. & C. Black, England.

Pole, Paddle and Portage. William Riviere; Little, Brown and Co., Boston.

White Water Handbook for Canoe and Kayak. Urban; Appalachian Mountain Club, Boston.

White Water Sport. P. D. Whitney; Ronald Press, New York.

Index

About the Authors

Gary Paulsen was raised in Minnesota on a farm adjacent to the immense northern wilderness areas. He has published many articles, T.V. scripts (Mission Impossible), and dozens of books on a wide variety of subjects, including fiction. One of his favorite subjects is the wilderness and its denizens. Paulsen and his family reside in a home in Northern Minnesota that he built from scratch where one can still see herds of deer foraging through the pine thickets.

John Morris writes with Pikes Peak and the Rocky Mountains outside his back window. As a Scout, he tramped other areas of Colorado. Morris did some "serious" hiking and camping in Vietnam when he was a motion picture team chief filming infantry operations. Since then, he's worked as a newspaper photographer and columnist, freelanced articles, projected movies, and worked as a stagehand in Colorado and California.